THE
RAREST
OF THE RARE

THE
RAREST
OF THE RARE

VANISHING ANIMALS,
TIMELESS WORLDS

DIANE ACKERMAN

RANDOM HOUSE
NEW YORK

Some of the essays in this work were originally published
in other versions in *Condé Nast Traveler,*
Life, National Geographic, The New Yorker, and *Parade.*

Readers interested in the poems written during some of these trips
may wish to turn to *Jaguar of Sweet Laughter: New and Selected Poems,*
where they will find a group of Amazon poems and one set on
French Frigate Shoals. They will also find there poems
about the Antarctic and other locales mentioned
in *The Moon by Whale Light.*

Library of Congress Cataloging-in-Publication Data
Ackerman, Diane.
The rarest of the rare : vanishing animals, timeless worlds / Diane
Ackerman. — 1st ed.
p.   cm.
ISBN 0-679-40346-9
1. Endangered species.   2. Rare animals.   3. Endangered
ecosystems.   4. Monarch butterfly—Migration.   I. Title.
QH75.A32   1995
574.5'29—dc20   95-8499

Book design by Oksana Kushnir

CONTENTS

INTRODUCTION

On the home planet, in the high latitudes, near the eastern edge of the North American continent, between two glacier-carved mountains, at the foot of a lake where humans balance at speed on knife blades, under gray skies, while ice pellets cover the ground with a thin layer of gooseflesh, in the waking-sleep of December, whose labored breathing is as familiar as a dozing spouse's, near a county airport, where steel mastodons land calmly but Canada geese circle in honking-mad wedges, among islands of urban forest browsed by white-tailed deer, in a cul-de-sac at the end of a key-shaped lane, behind a modest white house whose windows drink in the sky, one discovers a small part of one's address: that tilt of planet and mind we call winter.

Despite the cold, my backyard welcomes a riot of species. On two apple trees, mummified fruits hang like rusty bells. Although I cannot hear or smell them, I know that to the deer they are tolling with scent. A Japanese maple outside my study window has lost most of its leaves. The few lifeless, brown, twisted ones that still dangle have so little weight they're constantly atwitch and ashiver. On the hunched redbud, dry seedpods rattle in the wind like tiny gourds. Cardinals, chickadees, and squirrels use the interlocking branches of the redbud and maple as a highway. Occasionally they slip from an ice-jacketed branch, or tumble when the winds swivel fast. But they're used to seeing me behind the windowpanes, at a safe distance. I judge the direction and force of the wind from watching them. For warmth, they stand facing the wind, so it blows in the same direction their feathers or fur grows. Today the cardinals are puffed up like wads of cotton candy, and they're all pointing east.

Although I rarely spot field mice and shrews in the flesh, I often see them tunneling beneath the snow. Sometimes a rabbit or a groundhog strays from its nest. The five raccoons, balled up in the trunk of a half-dead maple tree on the north side of the house, wore a path across my lawn all summer, tumbled the garbage cans, and skittered across the roof. I know just where their den is—a hundred feet up in a gouged-out bolus of wood—because one pantingly hot summer day they crept slowly out of their nest and draped themselves on the branches to cool off. I'm not sure where the garter snakes have gone for the winter. Some years, at springtime, I find them waking indoors, so I suspect they've found a toasty bolt-hole in the walls or near the furnace. Three brown bats are hibernating under a house eave. Crows as big as eggplants weigh down the trees. Other birds visit the feeders, leaving footprint hieroglyphics in the snow. I miss the frogs and insects and spiders and butterflies that combine in warm weather to make a tapestry of fidget and color that stretches from belowground to the sky. I miss the flowers, whose buoyant colors and smells drench one's senses. But even in winter, many life-forms homestead this small piece of world.

From a bookcase by my desk, I pull out a copy of one of my favorite books, *The Home Planet,* a dazzling collection of photographs of Earth taken from space, and open it to a particularly beautiful shot of the Indian Ocean with a feathery smear of clouds above it: Earth at its most marblelike and blue. The oceans that gave birth to us support vast herds of living things—not least the phytoplankton, right at the bottom of the food chain, on which much of life on Earth depends. How can we allow something as large as an ocean to die? And yet, the Great Lakes are nearly dead. The Mediterranean is in its death throes. Some whales contain such high levels of poison from all the pollutants dumped into the ocean that even though they're living animals, they would qualify technically as toxic waste.

Leafing idly through *The Home Planet,* I stop at a picture of Earth floating against the black velvet of space. Africa and Europe are visible under swirling white clouds, but the predominant color is blue. This was the one picture from the Apollo missions that told the whole story—how small the planet is in the vast sprawl of space, how fragile its environments are. Seen from space, Earth has no national borders, no military zones, no visible fences. Quite the opposite. You can see how storm systems swirling above a continent may well affect the grain yield half a world away. The entire atmosphere of the planet—all the air we breathe, all the sky we fly through, even the ozone layer—is visible as the thinnest rind. The picture eloquently reminds one that Earth is a single organism. For me, the book contains visual mnemonics of how I feel about nature. At some point, one asks, "Toward what end is my life lived?" A great freedom comes from being able to answer that question. A sleeper can be decoyed out of bed by the sheer beauty of dawn on the open seas. Part of my job, as I see it, is to allow that to happen. Sleepers like me need at some point to rise and take their turn on morning watch, for the sake of the planet, but also for their own sake, for the enrichment of their lives. From the deserts of Namibia to the razor-backed Himalayas, there are wonderful creatures that have roamed Earth much longer than we, creatures that not only are worthy of our respect but could teach us about ourselves.

Some of those wilds I know personally, at the level of sand, orchid, wingless fly, human being. So each photograph is an album, a palimpsest, a pageant. There is Torishima, the little island south of Tokyo, which is the final stronghold of short-tailed albatrosses. There is French Frigate Shoals, the last refuge of the Hawaiian monk seal. There is Antarctica, home to vast herds of animals. While I look at a photograph of the Hawaiian Islands—puddles of ink on a bright copper sea—I remember the sound and rumble of humpback-whale song cresting over me as I swam. Humpback whales have had a civilization without cities, a kind of roaming culture, for many ages. They live in the ocean as in a wide blue cave. They pass on an oral tradition, teach one another their songs, abandon old versions, use rhyme. Our recordings of them go back only to 1951, but after more than forty years, the whales haven't returned to their original songs of the fifties. Just imagine the arias, ballads, and cantatas of ancient days that have filled the oceans with song, then died out, never to be heard again. Today we can visit the campfires of a few remaining tribes of Stone Age people and hear the stories they tell, stories marvelous, imaginative, and rich with wonder. But we will never know all the lost stories of the cave people. The same may be true of humpback whales. As I page through the book, I feast on habitats far-flung and dizzying. Life haunts every one of them, no matter how distant, dry, hot, salty, or sunless. The photograph of Africa reminds me of the giant animals caged forever in the past. The large animals we associate with Africa—elephants, giraffes, hippos, ostriches, and others—are dwindling remnants of the massive creatures that once flourished. *Indricotherium,* a relative of the hippo, measured about twenty feet at the shoulder and browsed on the tops of trees. A person standing beside it would barely reach its knee. There were mammoths bulkier than elephants, beavers the size of bears, jumbo elk with huge trellises for antlers, towering horses, bison as broad as a car. And, of course, there were Neanderthals, big, burly hominids, related to us. Were they a slightly different species, a competitor we killed off? Neanderthals survived in Europe, practicing burial rites and other religious rituals, for about seventy thousand years. Then *Homo sapiens* appeared, with their cave paintings and quick minds, and before long all the Neanderthals disappeared. When I look at the photographs of Borneo, Brazil, and New Guinea, I remember how the dynamic well of the rain forests has generated new life-forms. Our genetic safety net is woven from their biodiversity.

I set the book down on the table beside me in a puddle of sunlight. At one time or another, life has auditioned all over the earth. About forty million different species share our planet right now, and that seems like a cornucopia, but ten times that many have lived here in the past. Some scientists put the estimate close to fifty billion species. Because the human life span is short, record keeping recent, and our collective memory so poor, some assume that rhinos and elephants are forever, that we are forever. Evolution, that slow and steady plodder, will protect us through sheer sloth, won't it? Reassured by the logic of "If it ain't broke, don't fix it," we feel secure about the *gradualness* of time. Anyway, according to myth and religion, we are evolution's goal. But 99 percent of all species on the planet have gone extinct, including some of our close relatives. Just because we have evolved minds that crave order doesn't mean that nature is orderly. Evolution is a sleeping watchdog. It is possible for us to disturb it, or it may wake on its own. Either way, expect commotion.

The word *extinct* comes from the Latin *stinguere* (to quench), which is the verb of choice for killing a flame. Because we live on a planet hospitable to fires, which consume but also heat, we are obsessed with the notion of fires within our own bodies. This is not just a metaphor that came in with the Industrial Age's dynamos and furnaces; the ancients also wrote of fire in the flesh. When we say something is extinct, we mean literally that the flame in each and every cell has been doused. Yet we use *extinct* not as a verb but as an adjective attached to the verbs *become* and *go*. Even in our use of the word, we are confused about whether extinction happens to a species or is caused by that species. Subconsciously, we think of it as a supreme failure. We do not realize that extinction is normal. There have been huge die-offs in the past, when many species disappeared, discarded by evolution in a doodling with life-forms that may seem heartless, mindless, merciless, but is also unmalicious, intentionless, random. The high extinction rate at the moment is unique within our span of recorded time, so it surprises us; but mass extinctions are not extraordinary. What should unnerve us is that, in the past, large waves of extinction have always wiped out the culprits: when organisms were too abundant, dominating the earth and ruining the environment, they went extinct, with countless other animals. Then a new form of ooze or mouse started evolution all over again. So it's not that large numbers of animals haven't gone extinct before, or that nature cannot take care of itself. It's that when nature does, things start off from scratch in a new line of evolution, and that line may not include beings like us. Humans could be among the fossils other life-forms speculate about one day (if they speculate), puzzling over our tragedy as we puzzle over the dinosaurs'. The systems that now exist on earth have taken hundreds of millions of years to develop, but they could collapse around our ears, collapse rapidly and take us with them. That doesn't mean that all life on earth would vanish, but that it might be radically different. There have been times when anaerobic creatures ruled and times when aerobic ones thrived. Five deer leaped into my yard this morning, to eat fallen apples beneath the two trees by my study. With coats thick and dark, they looked like burros. There was a time when dinosaurs grazed in this same region, and I lament their passing. But if dinosaurs still ruled the planet, we would not be here. It was their extinction that made room for the small, timid, nocturnal mammals that led to us.

Even to the most pious disciples of the planet, there are many forms of the sacred, many rituals of devotion. Some people see nature as too holy to touch; they believe it should be allowed to run free and fend for itself, finding its own equilibrium, obliterating species willy-nilly. This fatalistic view sees us simply as one facet of nature among many other equally extraordinary facets; it may include a notion of God as an absentee landlord. Some people object to the way we "play God," choosing to save some animals and pull the plug on others. For example, should so much environmental money have been spent on the condor, whose role as a scavenger has been eroded by civilization? Some believe that all life is sacred and therefore all species must be preserved. Others argue that what is sacred is the mechanism of nature, and that one of nature's ways is to abort species that aren't adapting well, and to burn down forests as a means of refertilizing the soil. That makes more resources and space for other species. I happen to find koalas and pandas wonderful creatures, and for selfish reasons I would hate to see them vanish. But they rely on such precarious niches that their survival is doubtful. The koala eats only eucalyptus; a eucalyptus blight would be its doom. If we are driving species to extinction, we should stop. But if we're not at fault, should we interfere? For that matter, who owns an endangered species? What makes this issue more complicated is that it's no use protecting an animal by itself; you have to protect its entire habitat. When people contribute to the Save the Panda campaign of the World Wildlife Fund, the money actually goes to protect the habitat of the pandas, not just the animal.

If extinction is normal, then those who champion a laissez-faire relationship with nature have nothing to fret about. We'll lose some species, gain others. But people who cherish life on earth as it is now should be worried. The vanishing of so many other animals may indicate that we're not far from the brink ourselves. If we'd like our species to hang around for a while, we must be vigilant about what we're doing to other species, because evolution is a set of handshakes, not a list of winners. As Gregory Bateson points out in *Sacred Unity: Further Steps to an Ecology of Mind:* "The horse isn't the thing that evolved. What evolved actually was a *relationship* between horse and grass. . . . Thus the unit of what's called evolution out there is really not this species or that species. It's an entire interlocking business of species."

Dipping again into *The Home Planet,* I stop at a photograph of the Rio Negro, winding through the Amazon Basin in Brazil. My memory telescopes from space down to river level, where I snorkeled in waters dark and clear as quartz. A hundred miles southwest, the tannin-brown Rio Negro mixes with the pale Amazon in what's celebrated as the "Wedding of the Waters." I have walked and floated and slept along that river, whose banks teem with still-unnamed plants and animals. Going ashore is like entering a thick green vault. I remember the sting of fire ants, the fluorescence of a blue arrow poison frog. I was not then perplexed by frogs; now I am.

Frogs are disappearing all over the world. A friend tells me that when he was working in Panama, he discovered that traces of insect repellent on his hand could kill any frog he inadvertently touched. I've also heard that a virus, spreading across six continents, may be responsible for the demise of frogs. There used to be a beautiful golden toad in Monteverde, Costa Rica, that the local people enjoyed for years. Recently the people reported that none have been seen. No one knows if they're extinct or not, but they may well be. For most people, frogs aren't glamorous enough to be concerned about. But the speed at which frogs are disappearing should scare the hell out of us. As Paul Ehrlich has said, losing a species is like popping rivets on a plane's wing. You can pop an awful lot of rivets on a wing and probably the plane will not go down. But no engineer would want to be on that plane, popping rivets to see how many it took to make the plane go down. You might safely be able to pop as many as a hundred. But then you would get down to key rivets and not-so-key rivets. At what point would you have popped enough so that when the next one went, the whole contraption crashed? To change the analogy, think of chopping down a tree. When you first start chopping, the tree can heal, and it won't fall down. Chop a little farther, and it probably will survive if a big wind doesn't come soon. Chop a little farther, and it's going to fall down, no matter what. It's like that with life on earth. We're nibbling away at it without knowing when the point of no return will be reached.

It's tempting to think only large, attractive endangered animals should be protected. Most people feel their lives would be improved if more insects went extinct. But life on earth needs its insects, just as it needs its bacteria. People often think of bacteria as a cause of illness and death, and yet if we didn't have beneficial bacteria around, we would soon be gone. An array of biologically important bacteria has recently been identified in bat guano found only in specific caves; if we lost the bat colonies in those caves, we would also lose a lot of biodiversity we need.

A genetic palette of many colors, biodiversity is crucial to the survival of life on earth, and also to our health. In a burst of spirituality, it's tempting to picture this as a sort of rigid morality play: multitudes of plants, insects, and fish put on earth to provide the perfect antidote to specific human diseases. As digitalis (foxglove), quinine (cinchona bark), aspirin (willow), and thousands of other drugs have shown us, the rain forest's pharmacopoeia is indeed richly healing, and this is because of the deep kinship of all living things. A segmented worm seems radically different in shape, function, and form from a hydrangea, or an ocelot, or a college swim team. We picture life on earth as a feast of wildly distinct entities, but on the molecular level, they differ very little. They have cells, organs, fluids that contain similar stuffs, perform similar functions. Earth's chemicals can cancel, inflame, dilute, calm, deflect one another—as pigments do when you mix them—because, essentially, they're all composed of the same raw materials. A chimpanzee seems radically different from a human; but our genes differ from theirs by less than 1.6 percent. There is a deep-down kinship among all living things, not just spiritually, or morally, or through some accident of our being neighbors, but physically, functionally, in our habits, in our hungers, in our genes. Our common ancestor was life, and, at that, a rare form—earthlife—which developed its own basic shapes, symbioses, and motives. That will always make us more closely related to a panda than to a stone, and probably also more closely related to any facet of earthlife than to life-forms we may discover elsewhere in the universe. Superficially, an armadillo looks different from a kumquat; but Earth's bio-families are tightly related.

As more and more species become rare, angles of color will be deleted from this living kaleidoscope, reducing the possible combinations. Variety is not only the spice of life, it's the indispensable ingredient. So should we preserve the last remaining smallpox virus? "What good has smallpox ever done anyone?" people argue. "Think of all the suffering it's caused. Let's obliterate it once and for all." I'm glad it's locked up safe, and I pray it never escapes from its prison; but it may one day offer us an insight into, or solution to, a biological trauma we can't now imagine.

What could be thornier than the complex problems of ecoethics? I suspect there will one day be many university departments and think tanks dedicated to such debates. I only know that, for me, life is an unlikely and extraordinary happenstance, a fascinating predicament for matter to get itself into. I cherish life's variety and would like as much of it around as possible.

Why do we treasure what is rare? The word *rare* implies unusual quality enhanced by permanent infrequency. Rarity is not the same as scarcity, a temporary state. We come from a long line of cooperative creatures—shouldn't we value all that unites us? First, consider the part novelty plays in our heritage, indeed, in our cells. Our senses respond to *changes* in the environment. A lion standing in the grass isn't a threat until that lion turns its head toward you and begins an attack. If you have survived lion attacks before, perhaps you will recognize the first milliseconds of danger—the lion's eyes locking on to you and fixing you in space, the tightening of its shoulder muscles, the dropping of its head as it begins to sprint. When something changes in such a scene, our neurons signal a change. The body goes on alert. A silent whistle blows in the flesh. The body tenses to fight or flee.

Stasis, which we long for because it's safe and restful, soon bores us: the body slurs over the details. If nothing changes, the neurons can stay calm. Adrenaline isn't required. The blood pressure needn't rise. The brain needn't stir from its catnap. Otherwise, we would live in a snowstorm of sensation, a kind of sensory noise. We would be continuously aware of the feel of a watchband, a sweater, a pair of glasses. We would never be able to take anything "for granted," as we like to say. For life's racket to become a polite blur, against which food or danger looms, we must take it for granted. But we also crave the feel of our response to change, which shakes us wide awake and makes every detail of the world seem suddenly important, distinct, sharply defined. When something new appears, we assess it in depth, with all of our senses paying strict attention, just in case it is a threat, or a source of nourishment, or a harbinger. All at once, adrenaline pours, the pulse quickens, blood flows faster, the muscles contract and prepare for a tough workout. If we stand still and don't flee or pounce, all that welcome turmoil stays bottled up, and we feel ready to boil out of our skins. We feel a thrill that grows steeper with the magnitude of the threat or the opportunity at hand. Studies have shown that when an unfamiliar woman enters a room, the testosterone level of the men rises. Novelty excites us viscerally.

But it also excites us as an idea. What is life? we ask, knowing that the answer will come not as a headline but as an aggregate. Life is dewclaws and corsages and dust mites and alligator skin and feathers and whale's whiskers (as mammals, whales do have hair) and tree-frog serenades and foreskins and blue hydrangeas and banana slugs and war dances and cedar chips and bombardier beetles. Whenever we encounter something that is rare, we mentally add it to the seemingly endless list of forms that life can take. We smile in amazement as we discover yet another variation on an ancient theme. To hear the melody, we must hear all the notes. So we're drawn to new notes, notes our friends have not yet heard.

Sometimes it is difficult for us collectors of rare artifacts such as paperweights or buttons or paintings to understand that we ourselves are rare. We may be the rarest animal of all, and we are by far the most dangerous. We like to gloat about being at the top of the food chain, but the truth is that we jumped line. Other animals are faster, tougher, stronger, better armored. What we are is mindier. Our brains indulge in a form of mischief that, for lack of a better word, we call thought. We are among the rarest of the rare not because of our numbers, but because of the unlikeliness of our being here at all, the pace of our evolution, our powerful grip on the whole planet, and the precariousness of our future. We are evolutionary whiz kids who are better able to transform the world than to understand it. Other animals cannot evolve fast enough to cope with us. It is possible that we may also become extinct, and if we do, we will not be the only species that sabotaged itself, merely the only one that could have prevented it. Because vast herds of humans dwell on the planet, we assume we are invulnerable. In a sense, we are a virus that has swept over the world, changing and devouring it. Whether or not we are a plague remains to be seen. Because our cunning has allowed us to harness great rivers, to fly through the sky, although we were not born to, and even to add our artifacts to the sum of creation, we assume we are omnipotent. Because we have invented an arbitrary way to frame the doings of nature, which we call time, we assume we are immortal.

For the past years, I've been traveling to see some of the rarest animals and ecosystems. As a member of the species responsible for their downfall, I feel an urgent need to witness and celebrate them before they vanish. But my motives are also selfish: I ache to know how dinosaurs ran, what their skin felt like, what sounds they made, how they cosseted their young. There are little-known species alive among us now that have lived on the planet for millions of years longer than we have but will perish without our noticing them, without our chronicling their ways and habits. I find that thought unbearable. So many plants and animals are endangered that it would be impossible to write an exhaustive book on the subject. So I've chosen here to focus on three delegate animals (monk seals, short-tailed albatrosses, and golden lion tamarins), two endangered ecosystems (the Amazon and the Florida scrublands), and an "endangered phenomenon" (the migration of the monarch butterfly). They are some of the errands life is running at the moment. I couldn't resist tagging along.

For me, that has always meant observing the animals in their natural habitat while working with scientists who have devoted their lives to them. That usually requires at least a small pilgrimage, which I find nourishing in countless ways. But sometimes I find myself described as "a hard-core adventuress," to use one reviewer's words. Meant as a compliment, that emotional silhouette is far removed from my motives and disposition. I guess people associate violence and brutality with the wilderness and don't think of women as feeling at home there. When Giraudoux writes in *Ondine,* "A woman's hand, no matter how soft, can become a shell of iron when it protects a living thing," he means not that the woman changes into a Valkyrie, but that softness and strength are not incompatible. There is a strength one rises to in rare moments, a stretch of cunning or physical ability. And there is a strength one pares down to, a tundralike patience, self-denial, or determination. Both can occur as often in the inner city or on a college campus as in the Amazon.

At thirteen, I desperately wanted to be what I then thought was called an adventuress. It took me years to discover the true landscape of that word, with its night-prowling denizens and emotional quicksand. And it took further years to understand that I didn't mean "adventurer," either; I meant some sort of naturalist/poet who patrolled the wilds of the world and the emotional jungle of ourselves with snares made of sentences and darts tipped with wonder. There was a literary tradition to join, though I didn't suspect it at the time, which included stylish fiction writers such as Melville and Conrad, who had tramped through what Wallace Stevens would later call "the wild country of the soul," and also rhapsodic nonfiction writers like Loren Eiseley and Guy Murchie, and literate explorers like Sir Richard Burton, among many others. They electrified armchair travelers like me with their sensory caravans. Now movies and television perform that function for many people, but I still love to see the world through the handheld lens of a book, to add others' sights and insights to my own.

I love to sketch with words and try to make portraits of life in process, and to ponder things. Some overly solemn people, who seem to know too much about what nature is *for* to be able to enjoy it, feel that you can't be serious without being preachy, nor sincere without being earnest. Nature is indeed sacred and must be protected. We should all care urgently about the fate of our animals and ecosystems, and should work hard in their behalf. But nature is also great fun. To pretend that nature isn't fun is to miss much of the joy of being alive, and to deny the curiosity, restlessness, celebration, spirituality, invention, play, and other quirks that make us characteristically human. If I respect the unique ways of the elephant or the bower bird, should I not respect the unique ways of the human?

I pray there will be no mishaps on expeditions, and I always try to avoid discomfort. But there is no use pretending that it isn't good old-fashioned fun sometimes when you discover that you have to get really and truly mucky—reaching into a burrow to check an Antarctic prion, wading up to the thighs in ropy Amazonian mud, shuffling through guano thick as peas. Sometimes the filthier, hungrier, sorer, and more weather-beaten I get, the more I feel a deep-down child-of-the-earth radiance. Few things are as satisfying as meeting nature on its own terms, attending to its rhythmic demands, and then trying to snare it briefly in the net of the imagination, studying its gestures and moods, and making the drama that normally spins out in four dimensions pause a moment and roost temporarily in two.

When I read my notebooks later, they escort me back to people, places, and events I may never experience again. The cartography of life changes so quickly. It made sense that I felt this way about the albatross expedition, a difficult sea journey; but I was surprised to find that each of these expeditions filled me with that same bristling urgency. Although *I* was usually safe and comfortable, each day was a matter of life or death for the animals I traveled to see, so an alarm kept ringing in my chest. Returning home after each trip, I underwent a torrent of emotions, including privilege and wonder, determination to help the animals in whatever ways I could, and that special pang one feels saying good-bye, just in case, to war-bound friends.

THE
RAREST
OF THE RARE

MONK SEALS

*I*n the mythos of the folk who make their living
from the sea it is well known that hidden in
the dark pools of the eyes of certain seals are
spirits that call out to certain men. The Irish
among us, and a few Scandinavians who have
lived long at the edge of the sea, can hear the
message best. These seals, they say, are really
fisherfolk who were caught in some act
displeasing to the gods and were made to live in
hairy skins forever after and to wander at the
will of the winds and the tides. Once in a while
such a seal will save the life of a drowning sailor
and will then be released from its beastly
bindings. It will turn into a beautiful maid and
will be the sailor's wife, but there will be no
offspring from the union, and the old women in
the village will know the reason why. Always
dark-brown of eye and soft of body these
beautiful creatures are, and they lie awake in bed
when the full moon streams through the window.

And their feet are a bit colder than the feet of
ordinary women.

—*Victor Scheffer,* The Year of the Seal

In daydreams I have seen its face: a bulbous head covered in silvery fur, with black buttonhook-shaped eyes, a snout on which springy nostrils open full like quotation marks, tiny tab-shaped ears, a spray of cat's whiskers, and many doughy chins. On land, it drags itself with excruciating effort, or ripple-gallops like a four-hundred-pound slug. But the water sets it free to swivel and race. Powered by twin flippers at the rear, its torpedo-shaped body can outmaneuver a shark. Books say it grows to seven feet long. But the photographs show distant and indistinct creatures. There are no cozy details—the touch, the smell, the sound, the expressions. No matter how long I stare into the mental well of a photograph, using it as a point of departure, I cannot see around the corners of the paper, hard as I try. So I've been wondering what a monk seal looks and feels like. Will it be powerful? Most seals are, but these are uncommon seals. Indeed, monk seals are the most ancient of all seals. What does the ancient look like, anyway? In photographs, monk seals look young and unformed, with round, puppyish faces. Is that what the ancient looks like— all soft lines and curves, a single flowing and bulging like the planet itself?

At last, French Frigate Shoals drifts below us. Behind the thin white petticoat of its surf line, a long comet of aqua stretches into the Pacific. Most of the ocean coralled by the atoll is shallow, with a sandy bottom; the reef drops steeply away at the outer edges. The islands themselves take many different shapes and lie apart like a slightly scattered jigsaw puzzle. The changing colors of the ocean tell which ones are surrounded by coral heads or sandy shallows, and where deep channels run. But they could not be more fragile. A few seem large enough to house a small building, but others are tiny as sandboxes, and from time to time they actually disappear.

This horseshoe-shaped spill of islets and sand spits provides the last sanctuary of the Hawaiian monk seal, "a living fossil," some have called it, a seal so ancient, rare, and shy that it seems almost mythic. For millennia, monk seals swarmed through the Pacific, Caribbean, and Mediterranean. It was the first pinniped recorded by Aristotle, the first seal spotted by Columbus. Tame, shore-loving, and exploitable, monk seals soon were slaughtered in droves. We think of extinction as a horror locked in the mysterious sea chest of our past, something that happened long ago, not as a process going on right now. But the last recorded Caribbean monk seal was spotted in 1952. I was four years old, growing up in a small town in Illinois, playing in the plum orchard across from my house, and learning to count. I didn't know that an animal that had survived for fourteen million years was at that moment becoming extinct, nor that I would one day lament its passing, and that most people would see a monk seal only if it was flattened in a textbook or stuffed in a museum.

A few monk seals still inhabit the Mediterranean, but vanishingly few, and they're rarely glimpsed. Not long ago, two researchers, traveling across Morocco to study them, died when their jeep hit a landmine. So many governments have divided up the habitat of the Mediterranean monk seal that organized research is not feasible. And, in any case, monk seals are rattled by human doings—motorboats, airplanes, fishing, tourists. The calm and soulful Mediterranean of Aristotle, where sirens sang lonely songs, has evolved into a carnival of racket, fun, and commerce. The only hope for the entire genus *Monachus* lies with the remaining Hawaiian monk seals, which have found a remote hiding place. Even these seals are vexed by problems.

All the monk seal wants is to continue living in the ancient seas for which it's designed. But those waters are gone now. Pollutants, plastics, and fishing lines ride the waves, and hominids stomp along the beaches or race across the reefs. Indeed, a Loran C satellite-navigation tower dominates one of the monk seal's key pupping islands. Occasionally a pregnant monk seal does haul up onto a fashionable beach on one of the main Hawaiian islands. Ironically, although tourists may lie happily for hours, broiling in the sun, when they see a monk seal doing the same thing they assume it's stranded or in trouble, and they chase it back into the ocean. That simple act—hazing it back to sea—may kill it and its young. Monk seals choose a beach carefully, judging terrain and shallow water. Frightened by humans, a seal will look for another pupping spot, one with fewer people, even if it means a less ideal landscape. A female monk seal needs a shallow crib for her young, right offshore, where she can protect and nurse it. Deep water close to shore invites sharks, the silent marauders of the reef, which relish seal pups. It's not only callous or reckless people who are at fault. We have a tacit belief that life is motion, and so well-wishers sometimes love a beached seal to its doom.

Suddenly Tern Island materializes beneath us. A long, sandy aircraft-carrier-shaped island, it was used by the U.S. Navy in 1942 as an outpost during the war in the Pacific. On final approach, the pilots put on white crash helmets, lest a wayward bird hit the windshield and shatter it. Turning, we line up with a broad coral runway, cut the engines, and begin the slow-motion fall of the landing, as great flocks of frigates, boobies, and terns burst like flak into the air all around us. As we touch down, a second barrage of birds flies up—brown noddies, this time, shearwaters, and plovers—and in a cyclone of birds we come to rest at last before a long barracks, outside of which a plaque reads: "Tern Island, French Frigate Shoals. Population 4."

The refuge manager and three women researchers come out to greet us and carry the boxes of food we have brought with us into the field station. A Π-shaped building with two long corridors leading away from a large public room and a kitchen, it once housed dozens of GIs. Now most of the small bedrooms stand empty. The open dining room and recreation area (complete with Ping-Pong table, pool table, library, and VCR), and the separate storage rooms and laundry rooms give it the feel of a college dorm. Four hefty refrigerators dominate the kitchen, and the walk-in pantries are loaded with enough food and drink for many months of isolation. Water is collected on the basketball court beside the building and then purified. A small, hot "dry room" protects the station's medicines, as well as its word processor, Xerox machine, walkie-talkies, and other sensitive equipment. A generator powers the lights and appliances, but when someone needs to talk on the shortwave radio, lights must be turned off to save electricity.

I've come to French Frigate Shoals with William Gilmartin, director of the Monk Seal Project, to tag this year's pups and check the general health of the adults. William Curtsinger, a *National Geographic* photographer, has joined us. Gilmartin is a tall, thin, bearded man in his fifties, with thinning hair, enormous hands, and strong nose and forehead. Curtsinger is lightly built, blond, and forty-four, with a face lined by many years of working beneath sun and ocean. Gil's tan-and-orange T-shirt says: "Hawaii—I've found a home." Bill wears a T-shirt also, light blue, and without a legend. For a week, we'll be a team.

On expeditions, it's always wise to eat whenever one gets a chance, regardless of time or hunger. So when we find a pot of chili and rice in the kitchen, we sit down to a heavy breakfast. Then I drop my kit in my room, number 13, on the east side of the building. Bill and Gil have chosen rooms on the west side, with windows opening onto a courtyard full of brown noddies and wedge-footed shearwaters ("wedgies"). My windows, locked in the open position, face the beach and ocean. If it weren't for the angle of the guano-speckled panes, a fairy tern, debating with its reflection in the glass, would be able to fly right in and land on the wooden desk. A conga line of tiny ants wends across a dust-veiled mirror sitting atop a chest of drawers. Opening a warped drawer, I find more ants and quickly realize that they are everywhere; a handful even meander across the white desert of my bed. Like the geckos patrolling the wastecans in the dining room, the ants are harmless, and I don't mind setting my clothes among them. An ancient instinct makes me jump when a bug or reptile scurries unexpectedly near my hand. But I like being reminded what frail outposts we construct in the wilderness, as if plaster, metal, and linoleum really could keep nature away from us, even temporarily. Nature always waits awhile, then sends in its platoon of ant, gecko, bird, or beetle—the where-you-least-expect-to-find-them brigade, specialists in remote places. So I don't mind ants in my bed here, any more than I minded, only a week ago, finding a garter snake basking on a potted chrysanthemum at my living-room window in upstate New York. It's nice to be reminded occasionally that borders are arbitrary, and that absolute categories such as "outside" and "inside" can just as easily reverse.

Gil appears at my door, dressed in black spandex biking shorts, a ripped T-shirt, and a peaked hat. In one hand he is carrying a small notebook, in the other a large white plastic bucket marked TAGGING. "Ready?" he asks. "Don't forget the sunscreen." Reflecting off the coral sand, the noon sun can be ferocious. Only mad dogs and field biologists go out in it.

Bill, Gil, and I rendezvous at the boat dock, where we use an electric crane to lower an orange Boston whaler into the water. Our first stop today will be East Island, a long, slipper-shaped island six miles southeast of Tern, which once held a U.S. Coast Guard station. The ocean heaves and rolls. Timing it just right, we jump into the lurching boat as if onto a merry-go-round in motion, put on life vests, test our two shortwave radios, and then set out. After a bone-jarring, wave-leaping ride of forty minutes, we see a bright doily on the horizon, staying low but sliding closer. Composed entirely of coarse coral sand and pulverized shells, East Island is only about two thousand feet long and four hundred feet wide, and it doesn't rise more than eight or ten feet above sea level. Actually, it looks more like a callus or a kneepad than an island, and a brisk storm could dash waves right over it. Masked boobies, sooty terns, and Laysan albatrosses fly out to greet us as we pick our way among the coral heads, at last settling for a spot on the leeward side of the island. Bill fixes the stern anchor in the ocean; I slide over the bow with a second anchor and run up the beach to plant its steel claws in a small dune. Gil radios home that we've arrived at East. When we leave, he'll radio again. This routine gives the field station only a small parenthesis of information, a mental bracket by which to find us. But if something should happen to our boat, at least they would know where to begin searching.

Wading through the warm water, we carry buckets and gear on our heads like jungle porters and leave them in a heap on the shore. The sun feels hot as a branding iron on any exposed skin. There is no shade, and the irregular coral sand, like millions of small perfectly white teeth, reflects all of the sun's fury. Gil says researchers sometimes play the idle-hour game of trying to find their initials in the coral fragments. Stooping, I cup a handful and let thousands of tiny ciphers sift through my open fingers. Because they look meaningful, my mind struggles to arrange them. It is just a reflex. Our senses search for patterns, and when we find them it's hard to accept chance as the culprit. But only the random chiseling of water on coral has produced this textured sand of shocking beauty. For a moment, I can almost feel the tugging as my mind probes the coral for meaning, lets go, probes again, lets go.

Beside me, and all over the island, lie clumps of debris from the North Pacific—empty bottles, old toothbrushes, combs, a plastic baseball bat, thongs, and hundreds of handblown glass fishing floats in round or rolling-pin shapes. Crazed by sunlight, the floats sparkle in an array of trembling blues and greens. They're often signed in Japanese, and some clouded ones shine like crystal balls. At first glance, the island seems to have been bombed. But the shallow craters are mainly the caved-in pits of the green turtle, or burrow nests made by wedge-footed shearwaters.

A tall Loran C tower stands at one end of the island, and I follow its hour-hand shadow down to the beach, where it falls across the flanks of a large monk seal. Browner than I imagined, and molting in patches, the seal looks a little like an old horsehair couch someone has left by the curb. Its belly glows a pale chamois-color and its chest is green from algae. Lying placidly with its muzzle half-buried in sand, the seal snoozes as incoming waves swirl around its face, sudsing its whiskers. I think of drowning. Breathing is so regular and automatic for us, our air hunger so urgent, that we forget that other animals need air on different schedules. After the seal inhales and exhales three times in a row, its chest stays motionless for ten minutes. Then, lifting its heavy head, it sneezes with a wild twisting of the neck and settles back on the sand with a loud harrumph. Monk seals suffer from nose mites, which give them terrible sinus problems. Although they can use their webbed front flippers to scratch at the face and mouth, they can't reach the mites very well. So they sneeze often, loudly, and with full sinuses.

Two pups appear in the surf and start playing rough-and-tumble. I assume that such play teaches them skills needed for mating or fighting. Gil isn't sure. Little is known about the courtship rituals of monk seals. In fact, mating has been observed only twice—once in 1978 and once in 1982. Both events happened in deep water, and one of the accounts is iffy.

Strolling past a low dune, we come upon six large seals lying parallel in the sand. Their sheer size is surprising.

"Look at all those monks holding down the beach!" I whisper excitedly.

Bill laughs. "You think the island is going to levitate?"

Now a smaller seal, sleeping in the middle of the island, takes a few breaths, wakes up, and steam-shovels its way closer to the water, digging a long trench as it goes. Because they feed at night, monk seals bask in the blistering heat of the day, but they do like to dig down to a cool, damp layer of sand. In many places we find "tractor paths" left by monk seals that have dragged themselves to the water. If the treadmarks lie close together, the path was probably left by a large green sea turtle, also endangered. Almost 90 percent of all the remaining green sea turtles (the "green" refers to their fat, which has a green tint) nest on French Frigate Shoals. Seal flippers don't make contact with the sand as often as turtle flippers do, so the tracks look just a little different.

Gil bends his knees, rounds his shoulders, and sneaks up closer to the sleeping monk seals, checking to see if any are pups in need of flipper tags. The information researchers glean from tagging helps to chart the life cycles and movements of the animals and the progress of the rehabilitation program. Turning back toward me, he points to a small dark seal right at the end of the row. Monk seals molt each year, and for a while their new fur looks slate-black; this will most likely be a pup that's gone through its first molt. Opening the white tagging bucket, I remove a tool for punching holes in leather belts, two fraying kneepads, paper and pencil, a tape measure, and two yellow plastic flipper tags. The color tells which year the pup was tagged, the number code stands for French Frigate Shoals. Holes drilled in the tag also signify the year, so that even if the paint is washed away, the tag will still be readable. An open jaw about an inch long, each tag has a small knob at one end. It's a simple but ingenious design. I study it to see which end is up, which part goes in first, how the next part must follow. Holding a tag in the air, I rehearse the best wrist action for forcing the knob through the punched hole and tugging the device into place. Can I grip the tag with both hands to pull it through if necessary? I can. I slide on the kneepads and tie a blue sarong around my waist; the coral sand would grate my skin raw in no time. Then I hang the right flipper tag on the right side of my waistband, the left flipper tag on the left side. When the action starts, there won't be much time for thinking. Coiling up the tape measure, I tuck it under the legband of my bathing suit, leaving a few centimeters dangling so I can grab it fast.

Okay, I nod to Gil, and creep up behind him. Stealthy and alert, he hunkers down like a predator and sneaks right up behind the seal, climbs decisively onto its back, and grips its cheeks in both hands. Waking with a loud, gargling *baah!*, the seal begins rolling and squirming as I rush in, fall to my knees behind its tail, and try to catch the twin flippers flailing around in such confusion that it's hard to tell left from right. I grab one out of midair and press it flat on the sand while the other smacks my face. Sliding the punch along the webbing between the first and second digit, I find a good spot and press hard; nothing happens. The seal struggles and complains. Then, leaning all my weight into my hands, I push again and this time hear the click of metal on metal and know the punch has gone through. I remove it. The seal smacks me full across the face with its flipper, raking sand and blood from my forehead down to my mouth. Quickly, I grab the left flipper, press it flat on the sand to get my bearings, find the inside digit's webbing, slide the punch in about an inch and a half, and press again with my full body weight, straining from the effort. At last, metal clicks against metal. If this seal were part of the just-started DNA study, I'd be saving the plug of skin for genetic analysis.

"How ya doin'?" Gil calls from in front. Straddling the seal's back, he's not actually sitting on it but corralling it with his long legs, pinning its front flippers with his knees. Gripping its chins, he holds its sharp teeth away from him, which also keeps the seal oriented belly-down.

"At the tags," I call back, just as both flippers sail up and crack me under the chin, then slap me full-face from left to right, which knocks me back off my knees. I crawl into place again, amazed by the sucker-punch of the flippers. Each has five digits and can open to a foot wide or close up tight as a baseball bat. Both are driven by a single powerful muscle at the base of the tail, a muscle thick as a human arm. Now the flippers clap and roll like someone packing a snowball, and it's hard to tell which is which. I grab one, flatten it on the sand, confirm that it's the right-hand flipper, pull the tag from my right side, push its knob through the punched hole, and drag the tiny surfboard-shaped hinge after it. While I angle the tag so that it locks, the flipper dances in the air. At last I force the tag into place and make sure it's secure.

"One done!" I call to Gil. Sweat has begun to pour down my face, carrying sand and blood with it. The wet fur smells chalky-sweet. The seal complains in a loud, steady basso gargle as I pull the remaining tag from my waistband and start on the second flipper. Only minutes are passing, but they feel long and exhausting.

"Two done!" I call to Gil. Yanking the tape measure free, I slide one end under Gil's rump and into his right hand so that he can pull it to the tip of the nose; I pull the other end to the tip of the tail.

"One thirty-five," I call. He repeats the number. Then I take the tape measure and move to the right side of the seal, which eyes me warily. What big black eyes and long stiff whiskers. It has a cleft in its nose like a cat or a llama, and a soft cream-colored overbite. *Baaah!* Its resonant gargle seems to come from a great distance and by way of an echo chamber.

"Under the flippers!" Gil urges.

Watching out for the teeth, I slide the tape measure under the seal's chin, under the chest, and over the back just behind the flippers.

"One-oh-nine-point-five."

"That's it," Gil says, climbing off. The seal rolls onto one side, facing us, and paws the air with a flipper. As it does, we see four tiny nipples halfway down its fawn-colored belly, and a vaginal slit right under the tail.

Female. A precious pup. A grave threat to monk seals is how few females remain—too few for the species to flourish. This imbalance has so upset the workings of nature that males are resorting to a bizarre and ruinous behavior. On two of the main breeding islands, where the number of females is unusually low, a grisly phenomenon called mobbing takes place. As many as twenty males will attack and try to mate with one female. This may take several hours, during which time they gore the female's back, slashing the skin off, ripping the blubber right down to the muscle, in some cases even exposing the spinal column. Savaged, the female dies either from her injuries or from shark attack.

Mobbing, they call it, as if it were nothing more painful than a political rally or a peaceful gathering of kangaroos. Torture and brutality lurk in that euphemism. Because nature neither gives nor expects mercy, one often finds naturalists inured to violence. Our prime directive is not to intrude as nature goes about its ways. A skua has chicks that must eat, just as a penguin does. Still, it's painful to watch a skua stab a baby penguin to death and rip out its entrails. When I saw that happen in the Antarctic, I felt as if someone were yanking a steel cable that led directly into my heart. Nature is indeed "red in tooth and claw," as Tennyson said. Of all the qualities that define us, pity, mercy, and compassion are among the most remarkable. One sometimes hears of household pets being sympathetic, or of dolphins aiding drowning humans, but who can tell the motives of animals? As dolphin specialist Karen Pryor once quipped, "Maybe we never hear from the people dolphins carried out to sea."

One thing I find especially disturbing is that throughout the animal kingdom, although different species vary in their mating rituals, violence to females is the rule. Even among our closest relatives, the chimpanzees, females who refuse sex to males may be killed. In Patagonia, I saw a massive bull elephant seal assaulting one female after another along the beach. In each case, he ripped open the neck of the female, who bled profusely and bellowed in agony; then he crushed her flippers under his weight as he mated with her, and rolled over her pup, killing it. Evolution can be a cruel and merciless parent, in whom extreme behavior can be triggered by the slightest shift in circumstance. Of all the hazards facing monk seals, the toughest to outwit may be their own rash instincts. Female monk seals would not normally be slaughtered during mating; it's only because so few are left that the species is being sabotaged by frenzied males. A bonus of female pups would solve the problem. But how could that be achieved? Unlike crocodilians, which can choose the sex of their offspring by where they place the eggs in the nest, seals are slaves to chance. Therefore every female monk seal must be protected. Mobbing is so acute a problem that the Monk Seal Project has begun a treatment program to calm the males. The idea is to lower the testosterone level of the most violent offenders. At Sea Life Park in Honolulu, the curator of marine mammals, Marlee Breese, oversees such an experiment with four adult male monk seals, whom she refers to as the CRAMS (Convicted Rapists and Murderers). If the experiment works, it will curb the deadliest males long enough to bring the ratio of males and females back into equilibrium.

Moving to a polite distance, we watch the newly tagged pup roll over in the sand and return to basking as if nothing special had happened. Gil is pleased to find a female pup that's fat and healthy and full of spunk.

"How do you know which males to treat?" I ask, as we put the tagging gear back into the white bucket.

"It's important that we don't treat the dominant breeding males," he explains. "The dominant males probably give the females some protection from the groups of attacking younger males. The program seems to be working on the test animals. The next step is to go into the field with the drug and treat about sixty males at Laysan, one of the two islands where mobbing is the worst."

Half-dollar-sized quiverings in the sand take shape as small funnels, and I know baby green turtles are squirming somewhere below, wading slowly through their deep nest. Tonight they will struggle free and begin a long pilgrimage to the water. Three researchers at Tern Island regularly check their doings. When they find a nest of trapped hatchlings here on East Island, they excavate it carefully and take the turtles back to Tern to be set free by moonlight. Threading my way around the turtle craters and bird nests, I step over a small fishing float and plunge through a trapdoor straight down into a shearwater's nest, then tumble onto my knees.

"Who pulled the ripcord?" I ask. After climbing out, I kneel beside the cave-in, scoop the sand away, and look carefully inside in case a chick might be trapped; fortunately, the nest is empty. Bill nods thoughtfully. The island is a hidden maze of birds' and turtles' dwellings, and he will need to protect his cameras if he falls. From a distance, East Island had appeared flat as a sand dollar, but its gentle dunes rise high enough to hide sleeping monk seals, and as we continue our walk, we chance upon many more of them lying peacefully in the surf, always facing out to sea. Are they being watchful, I wonder? Are they oriented toward incoming sharks? Or does a seal relish the feel of the waves lapping at the whiskers, skirling around the muzzle, sudsing the nose? Unlike other seals, which tend to crowd, monk seals don't form large groups. They're more ascetic (hence their name) and haul out alone. Lying parallel on the beach at regular intervals, they seem separated by an invisible force—a kind of reverse magnetism. Today, the seals occupy all the beaches, but in spring the mothers nurse mainly on the south side of the island, where shallow waters ripple. Ten- to twelve-foot tiger sharks patrol the waist-deep water of the north side, on the lookout for wayward pups or birds. Spring is the albatrosses' fledging season, and sharks wait for naïve chicks to land on the water and then snatch them under.

At the end of East Island, we approach the spindly Loran C tower, which stands like a lightning rod. On it, a blue-and-white sign reads: "National Wildlife Refuge." How can a patch of sand as small as this be a refuge? What is it exactly that the seals, turtles, and birds are seeking refuge from? Predators? The changing blueprint of evolution? Us? Have we become such bullies that we've driven other creatures to awkward hideaways? Some of Earth's rarest animals survive only in the small cloister of a hidden atoll, or the dense asylum of a highland forest, or the rocky fortress of an active volcano. In a sonnet addressed to a loved one, Sir Thomas Wyatt laments: "They flee from me, that sometime did me seek." Do they now flee from us, animals that once shared our beaches and savannas? Or, equally worrisome thought, have we already wiped out most animals within reach, sparing only those that dwell in remote landscapes? The islands of French Frigate Shoals do not look like a refuge. In fact, they themselves seem to need dredging and bolstering. Perhaps we are confused about what a refuge really is—not a place as much as a willingness.

A battered child might find refuge with a grandparent. A resistance fighter might find refuge in a hayloft. All the refuge sign really identifies is a mood, a stubborn protectiveness. The extinction of these animals will stop here, it demands, on this small raft of sand. Not because the island offers much shelter, but because the slide to extinction that these animals are traveling must stop somewhere. Why not here?

Below the refuge sign sits a white wooden box with a latch door. I open it. Someone has tacked up a poem—"Walk Softly"—to celebrate the sacredness of the place. Inside the door, photographs show the original Coast Guard base. Small beetles scuttle over the photographs and for a moment the base seems to be bustling with life. The white skeleton of a spider blows across the hinge. Other evidence of the base still litters the island: teal-blue copper carcasses of machinery half buried in sand, sonabuoy containers, a heap of cement debris. Though such leavings probably don't bother the seals, they are an eyesore. Whenever Gil visits East Island, he carries one brick away with him and drops it at sea. It will take ages to dispose of the rubble at this pace, but nature knows no rush; why should he? In time his plan will work. He also collects washed-up fishing-line remnants because playful monk seal pups often get tangled in them.

A masked booby flies over and the ocean reflects pale blue across its chest as it glides low and lands near two mother seals with their three-week-old pups. Waiting in the shallows, another mother calls to her snoozy pup, and the baby baahs back in a slightly higher register, then waddles into the water and darts to her, otter-fast. Monk seals make quirky sounds—from stuttering grunts to high foghorn blasts—with mothers and pups sharing the greatest range of calls. Some seals have tiny patches of blond fur, which glisten in the sunlight. No one is sure how such curious markings evolved, but they help to identify individuals. Could there once have been blond or even spotted monk seals?

"Oh, look at that," Gil says, wincing. I follow his gaze to a pup that has no rear flippers left. A shark has chewed them clean away, leaving only a thick red stump.

"God, I hope it's not a female," Gil says. "If it is, we'll have to catch her, put a tourniquet on the tail, carry her to the boat, take her back to Tern, and fly her to Honolulu. Maybe she could be treated there and used for breeding."

Sea Life Park in Honolulu already has six females in their rehabilitation program. Ten years ago, researchers discovered that monk seals practice "fostering." If two mothers are nursing pups and the pups briefly stray, it's likely that the mothers will exchange pups. Either they can't tell whose pup is whose or they don't care. At first glance, this altruism may seem helpful. If there are few members of a population, isn't it smart for everyone to look after the young? But unfortunately, mother monk seals can't continue nursing forever. When a swap takes place, a younger pup may end up with a mother that has been raising an older pup. That mother would already have been nursing for some time and would not have enough milk left to raise the young pup. Weaned too soon, the undersized pup would not be able to feed itself. Those are the animals the Monk Seal Project takes to Honolulu to fatten up. Then they're released where they're needed, on a part of the Shoals where the population is low or there are too few females. Twenty-five females have been collected since 1984, and fifteen have been returned to the wild. The other ten died.

"Primarily of heart problems of unknown origins," Gil explains as he sits down on a large blue fishing float, balancing it underneath him as it tries to roll. "In the beginning we assumed all they needed was fattening up, but some have health problems we can't deal with. In a wild population, you always find some animals with health abnormalities." In a large herd, sick animals would not be missed; but in a dwindling herd, they're obvious and daunting. One problem with endangered animals is that their numbers are so low that it's hard to decide if an illness is random and to be expected or is caused by some new artificial pressure.

When Dale Rice and Karl Kenyon counted the seals in the 1950s, they found approximately 1,100 on the beaches of French Frigate Shoals, and it's believed that the islands' total population was two or three times that, since the seals don't all use the beaches at the same time. A count in 1977 put the total population at about 700 animals—down by more than 50 percent. In 1987, 474 seals were counted on the beaches, suggesting a total population of about 1,200. The birth rate has been continuing to increase over the last few years, but it's still dangerously low, and for some reason it dropped in 1989. An odd fact that may be relevant is that there is no word for "monk seal" in Polynesian, nor does the monk seal appear in Polynesian myths. In fact, little is known about its history. Perhaps there never were many monk seals in the South Pacific. We know more about their history in the Caribbean, where Columbus encountered tawny-brown monk seals on his second voyage (in 1494) and named them *lobos del mar* or "sea wolves." In 1707 a West Indian traveler wrote: "The Bahama Islands are filled with seals. Sometimes fishers will catch a hundred in a night." And in the Mediterranean as late as the fifteenth century the monk seal was plentiful enough to fuel a commercial fishery and give its name to a Greek city, Phocaea. But how many monk seals did the Hawaiian waters support? Were there great rookeries of them or only small strongholds? Did their extinction begin many millions of years ago because they abandoned the harem-keeping that other seals find so successful? We may never know.

What could be more serene than sitting on coral sand, while the sun mounts the sky, the monk seals bask, and the breeze blows the surf into a gentle lather. For a moment, there's no sign of all the commotion taking place to save these few seals. At Sea Life Park alone, every day, handlers drain the water from the female monk seals' pool, catch the six seals in nets, drag them up the steep cement walls, hold them down, and force-feed them whole fish. Orphan pups are too young to feed themselves. We think of hunger as a universal drive and teacher, but the young pups don't even understand that they must eat, and without help they will starve. At Kure atoll, a string of nearby islands that aren't part of the refuge, there is an enclosure where pups are fattened up, raised through their first summer, and taught to feed before being turned loose. Part of what makes monk seals so challenging to the people who work with them is that they pose so many different problems. There is the mobbing, the fostering, the human interference, the entanglement in fishing nets, the reluctance of pups to feed, the dwindling populations in some parts of the shoals but not in others. This morning alone, we have tagged pups, been ready to transport a shark-bitten animal, kept a sharp eye out for pups inadvertently orphaned by fostering, seen a victim of mobbing. It's animal by animal that you save a species. Not long ago, monk seals were considered disposable. The National Marine Fisheries Service insisted that they were a "relict species," as they put it, unsavable, a waste of time and resources. Outraged and saddened, John Twiss, now executive director of the U.S. Marine Mammal Commission, argued hard for the protection of these endangered animals, pointing out that they live "entirely within our U.S. waters." When NMFS refused, he pleaded directly with Congress, which gave him a small amount of start-up money for the Monk Seal Project. Only a few years later, this "relict species" has a slender chance. In the annals of extinction, that is a major accomplishment. Twiss considers it an object lesson in what can be done with little money but a lot of determination. It has not been an easy battle. That scarcity equals value is an absolute law of commerce. And, unfortunately, that's just as true of animals as of gold. Monk seals have been fought over in boardrooms by people of good and bad conscience, good and bad moral character. Many of the players have changed teams or changed animals. But with some funding, volunteers, new strategies, and an energetic proponent in Washington, the monk seals are managing to hold on. "It's possible that we will be successful," Twiss once told me. "It's just possible."

A mummified seal carcass, lying on the beach, looks too shriveled and battered ever to have been four hundred pounds of yearning and appetite, or even a rib cage and a tree of blood. Soon it will be tugged apart by the waves, snagged on the sand, split into minute pieces. Objects left in the ocean lose their hard edges and are broken up into formlessness. They become more like the ocean itself. In time, all things placed in the sea become the sea. The sea excels at certain tasks, such as sorting stones according to size, but mainly it reduces things to their constituent chemicals, frees them of the burden of form, returns them to the general flux of the universe.

A large male monk lifts its head, cocks an eye at us, snuffles, puts its head back on the damp sand, and closes its eyes. I wonder what they make of us shy humans strolling along the dunes, occasionally plunging through a wedgie hole, taking care not to disturb their slumber.

"We're finished here," Gil says. "Let's have a look over at Whale-Skate."

Collecting our gear, we return to the orange whaler, and Gil hands round canned walnuts, a bottle of lukewarm water, and small tart apples. Collecting the beach anchor, I carry it to the boat; Bill pulls up the sea anchor and Gil radios the field station that we're leaving East Island. Next stop is Whale-Skate, the easternmost of the southern islands, about three and a half miles east of Tern. Actually, it's two islands: plump, curving Whale and tiny semidetached Skate. Together, they stretch only about two thousand feet, and sometimes the ankle-deep channel between them floods or Skate completely submerges.

As we weave among the coral heads and finally inch our way to shore, a pup swims out to greet the orange whaler. So much shimmery orange must intrigue it. Slipping over the bow, I carry the anchor ashore, plant it, and wade back to the boat. Swinging around from the port side, the pup paddles toward me, and I sit down up to my shoulders in the water, to look smaller and less threatening, as it sneaks in close, twitching its nose and having a good look-see. For long seconds, its stares hard, and I talk to it in a high voice (I've noticed that most animals are more threatened by low voices). Casting a few more glances over its shoulder, it turns to grab one of the empty bottles bobbing beside it, tosses it in the air, nudges it with his nose. This pup doesn't need to feed itself yet, but it's never too early to practice. What feeding monk seals usually do is dive down twenty-five to four hundred feet on the reef, find a spiny lobster, and slap it on the surface of the water to break it, then eat just the succulent tail. Their diet also includes eels, squid, octopi, and some reef fishes. Popping its head up in the periscopelike way that seals do, the pup watches us, then has a rollicking good sneeze. Pups are troubled by nose mites, too, but they vocalize in a higher register than adults—when they sneeze they sound like tearing butcher paper. Tiring of the bottle, the pup swims toward me again, this time straight across the anchor line, which it lies on top of, paddle-flailing in a splashy commotion of flippers, until it gets bored at last and swims away.

A mother monk baahs to her black pup, which baahs back. For forty days she will tend her pup without eating. During that time, the pup will gain 175 pounds, but the mother will lose 350 pounds. At last, scrawny and famished, she'll go out on a feeding binge, then find a mate. Next she'll spend seven to ten days molting, during which time she'll fast once more. We find several slender nursing mothers on Whale-Skate, and a few fat new pups to tag. One of them has a large, angry abscess on its back. Taking a razor blade from his kit, Gil sneaks up on the pup, straddles it, and quickly lances the wound so that, cleansed by the salt water, it can drain.

Afternoon begins rouging toward sunset as we pack up and start back. Reflecting the shallow water, green-bottomed clouds float above us. All the horizons are thick with clouds, some minty, some blue-white, wrapping us round and straggling high to where gauzier clouds stretch. It's like sailing through a planetarium. The planet's roundness and the great dome of the sky become obvious. Soon Tern Island appears, and we put the whaler away for the night and head into the barracks for showers and dinner.

Outside my bedroom window, four monk seals laze in the shade of bushes clotted with brown noddies. One twiddles its rear flippers. Another lifts its head and splutters a baritone phrase that sounds like *bogs on bogs on bogs*. A third rolls over, stretches its cream belly longer and longer. The fourth, vexed by a bird, nips at it, then crawls under a tree heliotrope (*Tournefortia argentea*). A male booby whistles, as if through badly fitting dentures. While two of the women researchers cook chicken curry for dinner, they play a tape of Beatles songs, which fills the barracks with close harmonies backed by birdcalls. We eat communally, worn out from the day's heat and drama; then, while the regular staff settles down on couches in front of the VCR to watch the remake of *The Thing*, Gil, Bill, and I retreat to our rooms.

At sundown, the barracks grow dim and a trail of small fluorescent stars guides one down the hallway and around the bathroom's sink and side table. All of a sudden, the wedgies begin moaning—only a few at first, then urgent throngs of them as night pours its India ink into the shoals.

The next morning, I toss on an oversized T-shirt and head for the kitchen, where I find Gil somnambulantly making drip coffee. Bill saunters in a moment later, his eyes still scrunched up from sleep.

"Sleep well?" Gil asks us. "The wedgies keep you awake?"

"Not me," Bill says. "It sounded like a thousand orgasmic women. I smiled all night."

Gil laughs. "That's a new one. How about you?"

"I liked the racket, too," I say, rummaging through the cereal boxes to find one without swarms of ants.

Bill leans close, whispers: "Try the Shredded Wheat; they're individually wrapped." I pull a packet from the box, pour its contents into a bowl, inspect it carefully for wildlife, add milk.

"Didn't get into it as much as Bill, of course," I continue, "but I love my room. There's a fairy tern nesting on my open window. And the monks were having themselves a fine old snore."

Gil laughs, shakes his head. Bill cuts me a glance that says *Look over there,* and I follow his gaze to a colossal box of ear plugs sitting on a shelf. Staff and visitors alike seem to find the night noises a plague. Still dozy, I think of Boethius, who once advised his readers that it was wiser not to yearn for "wine at midwinter" but instead to relish wintry things. This winter, in New York, I'll relish the snow-djinns swirling among the trees in my backyard, but I'll miss the moaning of the wedgies.

After breakfast, we go out to check the seals on Tern itself. Hiding behind bushes and crouching low, we travel along the beach like three cat burglars. Everywhere we look, we find recumbent monk seals—by the old water tanks, under tree heliotropes, on the basketball court, tucked in the dunes, using cement curbs as pillows, with tail flippers hanging into wedgie nests. There is a graceful, hillocky rise and fall to their outline, a soft geography. In molt, they look as if they were putting on their old trousers but got tired and lay down to rest halfway through. When a monk seal's whiskers dry, they curl up into a mustache; when they get wet, they straighten out. Older animals develop gray whiskers. Sometimes they raise their tail flippers higher than the rest of the body and rotate them in a wringing-of-hands movement. They don't get sunburned, as whales do. They don't pass out from lying for many hours with their heads downhill. They have hips, but narrow ones, and they sometimes cross their rear flippers, play patty-cake, or make praying hands of them when they sleep. On an incline, they find it easiest to move by curling the tail around, making a crescent of the body, and then shifting their weight until they're off balance, rolling downhill into the water. We watch a large male slow-gallop down the beach, rippling its thick weight across the delicate pink five-petaled morning glories. Its insides seem to be moving more slowly than its skin.

Ruddy turnstones stilt along the tideline, picking at the sand, and sometimes at the whiskers of sleeping monk seals, which wake briefly and bark at them. Downy frigate chicks hang out of their eye-level nests like sleeping cocker spaniels. Red-footed boobies with blue beaks peer at us with their sharp eyes; as we pass, they make the sound of clocks being wound. Around a clump of bushes, we find a large female monk seal with "132" bleached into her fur (researchers use Lady Clairol). Her mouth, curved like a croquet hoop, sports a thick, wiry mustache above it, and a white feather has been trapped in her whiskers. Dragging her five-fingered flipper across her face, she scratches the feather away.

Two pups roll on the beach, making a snoring moo at each other. The sunlight sparkles off their wet fur, painting neon down their backs. As the smaller one rolls, its tan-gray belly looks soft as a fedora. A single blast of sunlight, sharp as a welding spark, shines off the larger black pup. They roll downhill to the water and tumble in the surf, letting it toss them any old which way. Muzzles colliding, they bodysurf the waves. Then a third pup joins them to bob like dark plums in the green syrupy shallows. Now they roll onto their backs like otters and arch their fanned tail flippers out of the water. Newly weaned pups love to cavort like this, but by the time they're yearlings they'll be less frisky and more languorously adult.

A brown noddy glides overhead, making a perfect infinity sign in the air, as we inspect the deteriorating sea wall. There are eighty-nine monk seals on Tern this morning, and they seem content to lie asleep on the sand, dreaming their slate-gray dreams.

As the days pass, we rise in darkness, dress by moonlight, and set sail as the sun begins blueing up the sea. Few things are sweeter than the cool damp morning of a scorching day on the ocean. We return often to East Island and Whale-Skate, two prime pupping islands, and always find new pups to tag, new adults to inspect and fret over. Disappearing Island stays submerged all week. But we visit Gin Island, Little Gin Island, Trig Island, Near Island, Shark Island, and my favorite, Round Island. Floating near the north center of the lagoon, Round lies almost four miles southeast of Tern and it is not easy to find, since it is less than two hundred feet long and, at its steepest, rises only four feet above sea level. All coral and broken shell, the island has no vegetation. It looks like a lily pad drifting across the sea. And yet it boasts the highest number of successful monk seal births per square foot of any of the islands. Each time we approach it, through a maze of coral heads and sandbars, we see it floating small and arklike in the distance, brilliantly lit by the sun, with at least a dozen monk seals basking on its sands.

Although we call our planet Earth, it's mainly water. We should call it Ocean. This becomes radiantly clear as we fly for three hours over the plunging, misnamed Pacific, en route back to Honolulu. It's no use trying to fathom the ocean by studying a map or a globe. Anything our eyes can devour in a single gulp seems small and tameable. On a map, the whole Pacific Ocean looks no larger than a football. Maybe we should judge size not with our eyes but with our sense of time. As astronaut Paul Weitz once said of the Pacific, "When you're traveling at four miles a second and it still takes you twenty-five minutes to cross it, you know it's big."

Far below, the ocean slides along like endless yards of dull fabric. How can the birthplace of all life on earth—a realm of risk, terror, chance, and sunlight—look lifeless, boring? Our eyes fail us when we stand back too far. What we gain in perspective we lose in the polite blurring of details. Without the details nothing can be known, not a lily or a child. Looking down through ten thousand feet of sky, as if through the invisible pleats of history, I try to imagine the busy ocean below, which surges and leaps, froths and strains, contains rowdy fish and mammals, bustles like a souk in Marrakech. Ingenious hucksters haunt its coral reefs, eager to con passersby clean out of their cells. Large, muscle-bound thugs prowl its shallows and depths. Everything is up for grabs. Its sands bubble with skates, flounder, starfish, and sea urchins. Some of its inhabitants are as well armed as assassins. Others rely on armor plating, athletic ability, sonar, or illusion. Whales and dolphins mind its hinterlands, chatting and singing. Some of its creatures come to life, mate, give birth, and die without ever moving more than a yard or two. Others travel halfway around the planet, following their food supply or a yen for warmer temperatures. It contains valleys and rivers and great hulking mountain ranges and raised shallow platforms and precipices and chasms. In some places, there are ceilings of ice; in others, lava geysers or honeycombs of rock. It is not silent, but all atwitter and abuzz, full of animal clicks, moans, squeaks, and cater-wauling, as well as the relentless gnashing of water against coast.

Seen from a great height, the ocean appears flat, silent, and blue—a blue so turbulent and dark. The sea looks blue because it reflects the sky, but it's always a deeper blue than the sky itself because it doesn't reflect all the light. Some of its color also comes from the seabed. In the ocean, light falls from above as "down-welling light." Some fish, squid, firefleas, and other creatures make their own glow. But mainly light cascades over them. You need to be under the skin of the ocean, part of its gelatinous fathoms, to find illumination. When we look down on the ocean, it appears opaque. All its fascinating life-forms and geography are hidden, which leaves a mental void that quickly fills with imagined terrors. Therefore many people perceive the ocean as another form of night. And yet we are also drawn to the ocean; we like to vacation beside it, staring for countless hours at its hypnotic pour and sweep. It's both mesmerizing and narcotic. An impulse ancient and osmotic connects our fluids with the ocean's. I suppose we feel drawn to it because we ourselves are small marine environments on the move.

Islands bloom on the horizon, and we fly straight toward the center of the Hawaiian archipelago. First we pass over Niihau, a large privately owned island that's a cattle ranch. Monk seals haul out on its beaches, but the island's owners won't allow researchers to step ashore to monitor the seals, so no one knows how many use the island, what sex they are, or if they're healthy. Lehua, a tiny crescent-shaped island, floats off its eastern coast. Then the large island of Kauai appears, and a little later we land in Honolulu.

After a week of riveting calm spent on nature's timetable, the sensory blast of Honolulu hits hard. Bidding farewell to Gilmartin,

Curtsinger and I fly to Kauai and rent a diving boat to take us out to Niihau. Even if we can't land on its beaches, we might be able to glimpse monk seals from offshore. After a three-hour sail through choppy waters, we arrive at Niihau, the Forbidden Island, as some call it, and scout its north shore for basking monks, but find none. It was a long shot anyway. The towering crescent of Lehua looms half a mile across the channel, smooth and brown, with white specklings of guano. Long fingers of frozen lava stretch down its sides to the sea. Only one cloud haunts the Wedgwood blue sky—a large oval hanging directly over the island looks like a scar left by a knife wound. We head for the crescent's shallow reefs, to snorkel in one of several spots favored by divers. Seabirds work the thermals and the ocean pours metallic blue and green as we drop anchor on the south side about a hundred yards from shore. At the bottom of steep, twisting layers of rock, a weather-beaten hut sits on a cliff. Below and to the right of the hut lies an oyster-shell-shaped cave, partly above water, with a small lagoon in front of it. Sunlight dances like flame across the roof of the cave. Putting on a mask and fins, I slide over the side into twenty feet of water and find coral heads trembling with brightly painted fish and shifting spears of sunlight. The bottom is a maze of lava rock covered with oblong gouges where sea urchins have gnawed rock away, using their six teeth.

Heading for the sea cave, I enter a small commotion of water and light. The surf frets the entrance to the lagoon, where bubbles shake like beads hanging in the doorway of an opium den. Passing through the bubble net, I find a calmer, gourd-shaped lagoon, whose sandy bottom churns fifteen feet below. How silty the water is, thick and grainy. Ahead of me, a long, gray shape maneuvers. Suddenly it turns, comes closer, and stops six feet in front of me. Staring me straight in the face is a large monk seal with black eyes and thick whiskers. Heaven only knows what may be going through its mind. Perhaps something like: *Funny place to find a primate.* Eyeing me carefully, it pauses, then dives under me, rolling over as it does, comes up in back, eyes me again, and swings to my right. It doesn't seem to be using its flippers at all and barely moves its body, and yet it darts around at quite a clip. Two more seals appear from the curtain of bubbles, rolling tightly together. Then another monk seal swims underneath me, looking up at me the whole time by turning its neck right around like a ball turret, swimming forward but looking backward. It rolls onto its back and swims along the bottom below me, with its front flippers lying quietly against its chest as if they were tucked into vest pockets. Stopping ten feet away, it surfaces and considers my face. Then it turns slowly and swims toward the cave. Now the tussling couple reappears, biting and chasing each other. If I could rub my astonished eyes I would as five adult monk seals swim around the lagoon, in front of me, in back of me, at the surface, below me. What a dazzling spectacle. I am right in the middle of a monk seal fantasia. They seem no more bothered by my presence than they would be by that of a jellyfish floating above them. I think it is because I have large eyes (magnified by the face mask) and am watching them that they don't actually toy with me. None of the seals have flipper tags, so, unless they've seen humans on Niihau, I may be their first hominid. By now I am able to identify the couple as male and female. Occasionally they surface and baah loudly at each other; then the female darts away and the male joins her in a swirling subterranean dance. Bubbles trail from them like comet tails as they glide and spin, occasionally swiveling their necks to nip and bite. Before I have time to think, a new drama unfolds. To escape, the female dives to a jagged corridor of rock at the bottom that is just wide enough to hold a seal. The male follows her at speed, bites her flank, her tail, then tries to reach over the sharp rock. Huddled tight as a letter in a slot, the female pulls in her head and tail. At last the male sees an opening, grabs her back below the neck, and drags her out, forcing her belly-down on the sandy bottom as he mounts her. She goes suddenly passive. It lasts only a minute, but to me it seems ages as I float above them, frozen in amazement. Wonder is the heaviest element on the periodic table. Even a tiny fleck of it stops time. *I am watching monk seals mate,* I tell myself twice, as a complete sentence, because it is an astoundingly rare event to behold. The two other recorded sightings were vague and incomplete, and I feel lucky indeed. Most likely the pups I saw wrestling in the surf at French Frigate Shoals, tumbling and nipping like this adult couple, were practicing courtship. When the male releases his grip, the female bolts, and he chases her. They surface and one of them barks a short, gargling, wide-mouthed protest, to which the other answers with a loud, foggy bleat.

Night will be falling and the long trek home is best done in daylight, so, reluctant but happy, I fin back to the boat. What an array of monk seals I've seen. There is something sacred about seeing them, the last of a dying race of monks, swimming through underwater caves in a cathedral of light. When we hoist anchor and set sail for Kauai, we salute the sea cave I now think of as honeymoon grotto. Two monks are still swimming somewhere inside it. One large adult, hauled up onto the rocks rimming the lagoon, dozes peacefully near a pup. The courting couple continues swiveling tightly together among the coral heads. Over and over they roll, spiraling gracefully through the water. May their offspring flourish and be female. Standing at the stern as the boat gathers speed, I watch until the crescent island grows shorter, the shining monk seals become indistinguishable from smooth wet stones, their boudoir cave disappears, and all that's left are the indecipherable gestures of the sea.

IN THE AMAZON,
WHERE THE SUN DINES

*I*s there anywhere on earth that fires the
imagination the way the Amazon does? Even
when I was little, a pint-sized would-be explorer,
I dreamed of seeing its thick realm of vines and
snakes and gorgeous flowers and stealthy jaguars
and feather-clad Indians and piranha-studded
rivers and gushing green jungle. It took thirty
years for that dream to materialize in all its
lavish splendor. But, by then, the huge ecosystem
of the Amazon was endangered. The time I spent
cruising along the Amazon was an experience
both dizzyingly sensuous and deeply spiritual.
There was so much life at every level that my
senses felt almost bruised from the overload.
How could it be otherwise, seeing Nature at its
most luxuriant, teeming, and wild? It was like
entering the original Garden.

On Halloween, we drop anchor at Altar do Chão on the Rio Tapajós, a beautiful clear-water river, one of the tributaries of the Amazon. It is so wide, one cannot see its distant shore, only the shudder of its gray skin and the faint blue of the horizon. A white scimitar beach sweeps around a peninsula and tiny frogs hop near the tideline. Strolling through the nearby forest, we find large sandstone boulders ribboned with lavender; a stand of rubber trees, scored for their latex ooze; and a breu tree, whose resin, cousin to frankincense and myrrh, seeps fragrance and burns slow and aromatic. At eye level, on a slender tree, sits the top of a small bleached skull. I lift it down, look closer at the two sharp incisors, and offer it to David, a savvy ecologist, who has joined our cruise ship's scientific staff after a two-month botanical expedition deep in the interior of the rain forest. It is some sort of carnivore, but what? Cat? Dog? Otter? Raccoonlike animal? In the back of the skull, a small perfect bullet hole leads from one world to another. When David finds the mandible lying in the grass nearby and puts the set together, his face blooms with delight. It is the skull of a sloth, and he collects skulls.

Soon Zodiacs begin arriving from the mother ship with fixings for a barbecue of fish, sausage, steak, ratatouille, potatoes, rice, even mango chutney. One of the Filipino crewmembers takes out his guitar and a small group of men and women begin to sing in Tagalog. As the sun turns to red caramel behind pink and lavender clouds, people gather around a campfire whose whumping flames sound like wet sheets being shaken in the wind. After dinner, a few of us take snorkeling gear and an underwater lantern and prowl around the riverbed in darkness. Except for the occasional stingray, there is nothing much to fear in the warm fresh water as we watch for fish, shrimp, and shell. Small eels slither through the sand, carving sinewy trails. Other creatures have left hieroglyphics, but we cannot read them. Submerging in snorkeling gear, I drink a slow savory mouthful of the river, which tastes both tinny and soft, as if it's been stirred by water hyacinths. In the glow of the lamp, a brown petrified sail drifts into focus: a large clam lying on edge in the sand. Feeding along the bottom, the clam looks like a yacht setting out in the slowest race on earth. When we turn the lamp off, we can see the sharp, flintlike moon twisting its bright knives through the water and tossing onto the waves small garlands of light. Stars begin to drift overhead and shower their glitter on the water.

Later, as I lie in my narrow cabin, my thoughts begin to roam over the past week. For seven days we have been cruising a river that extends not just in miles but in time and imagination. The Amazon region is the largest tropical rain forest in the world. The river drains 20 percent of all the world's fresh water into the sea. Nowhere else is there so much life per square mile. Fifty thousand species of plants and fungi, a fifth of the world's bird species, three thousand species of fish (ten times as many as in all European rivers put together), and millions of species of insects share its tangled layers. The largest snake in the world, the anaconda, and the largest beetle, the dynastes, dwell here, along with other giants. From its richness, we have extracted cacao (for chocolate), rubber, quinine, Brazil nuts, chicle (for chewing gum), and an array of heart medicines and anti-cancer drugs. But tropical rain forests are being destroyed at about ninety-five thousand square miles per year; unless something is done, it will all vanish in my lifetime.

We began our journey in the remote reaches of the river, drifting with the current through a view of Nature carnal, green, and radiantly renewing, moving closer each day to the civilized deliriums of twentieth-century life, the duty-free emporia of Manaus, the neon carnivals of Rio. The river flows in only one direction, like time, and appears to be seamless. But up close one finds a lightly feathered surface, a plumage in which there are small puckers, rapids, and backwaters—also like time. Most Brazilians live on the civilized outline of their country, not in the wild chaos that inhabits the heart of Brazil.

In addition to the expedition's leader, Iain Prance, a world-class botanist who is head of Kew Gardens in London, there are other naturalists, and Mo Fortes, a famous and somewhat notorious Amazon guide who grew up in one of the small river towns. Each day, we rise early, often before sunrise, and climb into lurching Zodiacs to hear the rain forest waking up; prowl along the tributaries; visit Indian villages to trade, watch dances, have our ship's doctor attend the ill and leave medicines; talk with the river people; and, my favorite, take walks into the vine-thick jungle, under canopies effervescent with life. We began in Peru, passed swiftly through Colombia, and now are deeply in "Brazil, where the sun dines," as John Donne wrote, and the equatorial sun scorches body and soul. It doesn't feel or look like the Temperate Zone sun, whose rays, because of the tilt of the earth, strike at an angle, have to pass through a lot of atmosphere, and wash out a bit when they hit the ground. At the equator, the sun shines straight down like a heat lamp, focusing its energy onto a smaller space. It is possible to get a sunburn right through light clothing, and night doesn't dally: it cascades all at once, a black velvet curtain tumbling down.

One morning, Iain returned from the local Ticuna village with a strange tale. Four people had died mysteriously in the village that week, and the villagers were in mourning. Iain offered his condolences, as did we all. We were bringing them a repaired generator and a supply of medicines. They welcomed us warmly but explained that it was not a happy time for them. A community of two thousand, they are part of the most populous tribe in the Amazon (about seventy thousand). They are petite and have sharp cheekbones but otherwise soft features, straight black hair tied back with barrettes and ribbons, and a startling smile—they file their teeth to sharp points to mimic piranhas. Famous for their arts, they showed us animal carvings in whose simple lines and glowing resin shone a candor and unselfconscious joy. Is it naïve art? If it is naïve to marvel. Often the children tie ropes to the carved animals and drag them through the streets to play. There was some confusion about the people who died. They were poisoned by a forest plant. But was it an accident or was it suicide? The suicide rate is very high among the Indians here, as it is elsewhere. The river is their home, but it is also a quick slide into the twentieth century. The chief of that village has been wise with the money he's made from tourists, spending it on medicine, schooling, and other village needs. One of the first things they wanted was electricity. When boats sail by, they are covered in lights. The villagers wanted the ship's people to see lights on the riverbank and know there was a town there, an established people. What they make of us is hard to know. We find their ways strange, but to them we are probably another natural component of their environment, one with its own rules, taboos, and private dramas. We are pasty-faced giants who prefer to live in cold rooms, who dress in long-sleeved clothes in the hot jungle and are forever spraying themselves with the scent of pine and peppermint, and whose faces flush like cooked fish after a short walk. Only adults from our ships visit them. They said, "Good heavens, you have a very strange culture. Doesn't anyone in your culture have children?"

At one house, a man brought out his wares, including two live yellow-footed tortoises, whose heads and tails had been forced back inside the shells and held there with sticks. All shell, the tortoises looked like giant netsuke. They might know that torment for weeks or months, awaiting the cooking pot. So we bought the two tortoises, to set them free at a safe distance up the river. Among the many wares for sale there were no dolphin parts. In Belém, down the river and further along in civilized time, we will find dolphin vulvas and penises for sale in the voodoo market. But on most of the river the dolphins are protected by elaborate myths, and no one hunts them. Like the mythic silkies of Scottish legend, dolphins are thought to come ashore and make love with young women from time to time. So an illegitimate child is said to be the child of a dolphin, and if you kill a dolphin you may be killing your own father.

On the table beside me tonight stands a pot of hot tea made by crumbling and steeping the bark of *casca preciosa*, a fragrant relative of the sassafras. It has a bouquet that scents the mouth, the hair, the room, that washes up over your face as you drink. Sipping its sweet, violet-scented narcotic as lightning begins to prowl behind the peninsula, I drift into a river of dreams.

By early-morning light, we set out in our Zodiacs, and soon we pass a woman sitting on a caustic-sapped log, *açaú*, literally, "that which burns the asshole," to wash her clothes in the river in the ancient way, though she uses a twentieth-century plastic scrub brush, which she has probably bought from one of the itinerant peddlers who travel up and down the river, selling salt (used for drying fish) and other staples and household goods. A praying mantis flutters into the boat. It is a small brown-and-white insect with protruding eyes, horns on its back, and long waving antennae in front. Its jagged poise is beautiful as it preens its long legs and makes slow and purposeful gestures. Fish leap from the water, fleeing predators. What a perfect getaway: hurl yourself straight into another dimension of reality, as flying fish do, and suddenly appear elsewhere and elsewhen. Three little girls row out in a bark canoe, flash hundred-watt grins, stand up suddenly, and jump into the water. One man on shore holds up a pair of binoculars and watches us, the exotic primitive tribe madly unfolding colored ponchos from their packs and squirming into them because rain has begun to fall like a wall of rubber. Children go on playing in the shallows; adults continue to swim, wash clothes, mend their boats and nets. It is only rain. This is a rain forest. Holes in the banks, carved by walking catfish in April or May, when the water level rises as much as thirty feet, make the mud look like a condominium of birdhouses. On some of the lighter trees you can see the dark waterline, and many trees have large, exposed root systems to grab nutrients directly from the seasonal flood.

In a tall, bushy-topped tree, a dozen hanging nests belong to oropendolas, birds that have a symbiotic relationship with a number of animals. They like to build their nests in trees where there are hornets' nests so that the hornets, which attack parasitic botflies, will keep them from the chicks. The oropendolas also allow cowbirds to lay eggs in their nests so that the cowbird chicks, which are born with their eyes open, will eat botflies, too. The siren song of the oropendola is so complex and willowy that river people often build their houses under an oropendola-inhabited tree. The song begins with a wet, two-stage warble, a liquid undulating smooch, part throb, part Moog synthesizer, and ends with the sound of a debutante throwing kisses underwater. *Birds of*

Colombia, by Steven Hilty and William Brown, scans it as "EEE-eee-D'D'Clock-agoogoo," but there is a mellow swoon in the final stages of the call that's seductive and magical.

Behind the Zodiac, the wake makes a perfect white water butterfly, wings outstretched and outlined in spray. The forty-horsepower engine gnaws like a buzzsaw, and its blade cuts through the reflection of trees in the opaque brown water as we scout the shore for birds, mammals, unusual plants. Along the bank lie logs waiting for high water and their trip to the mills, when they will be laced together in a large raft. A gash of light splits the water about ten yards away, as if a window sash has been thrown open, and then a pink dolphin surfaces and dives back through its window. *Oh!* I say: like the dolphin, I take a small gasp of air. Suddenly four more pink dolphins arc out of the water in front of us, and one surfaces right next to the boat with a small, explosive breath. Close to the ancestral whale, these dolphins and their platanistid relatives are frequenters of the Amazon, Ganges, Yangste. On their snouts they have short, tactile whiskers to feel for food. At the riverbank a striated heron stands with its back to the sun so it can hunt in its own shade. A brown sphinx moth with a bright orange body planes low at eye level, followed by a heron, floating pterodactyl-slow with long rippling neck: a stately white apparition. We spot a tassel-topped tree, *Triplaris,* which has hollow stems inhabited by stinging ants whose venom feels like hot wires. Lianas drip from the trees, anchoring in so many places that it is hard to fathom where the vines begin and end. The brown river bubbles gently; fish leap up, mouths open. We hear the sound of a trigger cocking, then the low mournful call of a patoo, a bird that can mimic dead sticks. A sun bittern flashes the big false eyes of its wings. Trees, swaddled in leafy vines, look like the feathered feet of huge owls. A kingfisher sounds like a child's rubber squeaky toy. It is early morning on the Amazon, and the birds sing their territorial anthems. They do not mean to be beautiful. They cannot help themselves. A capuchine (organ grinder) monkey moves through the top of a tree, sampling fruit and dropping what doesn't appeal to it, like someone testing chocolate bonbons. The sound of fingers dragged across a rubber inner tube comes from a bird. When we drift near a fisherman and his son in a bark canoe, David calls in Portuguese: "Good morning, sir. How's it going? Catch much today?"

The man smiles, gestures to the bottom of the boat, where freshly caught fish lie in a pool of water. "Good morning," he says.

"The people would like to have a look at the fish, if that would be possible," David asks in a respectful and polite subjunctive, on behalf of the collective desire of our boat, "the people," as he puts it.

The man grins and maneuvers his tippy boat next to ours.

"You've done well this morning, eh? *Aruaná, peche cascudo, curimatão, piranha.* Would it be possible to see the bony-tongued fish there?"

The man lifts the long, glistening fish in his hands. How Himalayan his lined face looks, a reminder that he shares genes with Mongols and many other peoples.

"I'm obliged," David says, and opens the complex and fascinating mouth of the fish, whose tongue is a thin bone. Bony-tongued fish like to eat monkey feces and often wait under a tree where monkeys live. Then David picks up an armored catfish, which has a shovel nose, strange upside-down omegas for pupils, long sensory barbell appendages on its face, and beautiful black stripes. Next David takes a reddish cashew piranha from the old man, opens up its stomach with a machete, and smears the contents onto his finger to reveal that it holds mainly fish scales. The piranha nips at other fish to feed. It is not by choice the voracious carnivore of gothic stories and monster movies; unless it is cut off from its usual food supply and is famished, as it might be in an isolated swamp or lake, it is happy enough nibbling scales from fish. David hands the fish back to the fisherman, who generously offers us some to take back with us, if we like.

"No, thank you. That is kind of you," David insists. "We are glad to look at them, and learn about the life of the river. But, if it wouldn't be too much trouble, I know we'd enjoy seeing how you use your net to fish."

The man's face lights with the pride of shared craft, and he picks up the net as if it were a hemp skirt hung with lead weights, secures one end in his mouth, and tosses it in an arcing spiderweb over the water, then watches it sink down into the shallows where fish wait. There is wonderment in the shape the net takes through the air, its calm descent, how it vanishes into darkness. And the man watches our faces, smiles, drags the net back, and tosses it again and again. A small bird with a bright yellow belly like a dollop of lemon pudding perches on a branch and calls, *Bem ti ver!* ("Good to see you"), its name in Portuguese. In English, the bird's name is onomatopoeic, too: *Kiskadee!*

Later, at a peddler's boat, we stop to chat. Inside there are stacks of bananas and bagel-shaped bread; large fillets of salted fish are drying on the roof, swarmed over by flies. He offers us the hospitality of his house, just up the hill, behind which there is a large lake; his wife shows us her turtles, parakeets, and two hives of African killer bees, which she keeps for honey (each hive is locked inside a log that opens and closes like a sea chest). Digging at the base of one of the manioc plants in a field, she exposes the root to show us its long white fingers. Painted on the front of her house are the words CASA FEEM DEUS. I ask her what *feem* means, and she looks puzzled, laughs, struggles to explain. After an awkward moment, we laugh, too. *Feem* is a contraction of the words *fé* (faith) and *em* (in). I have come from the wilds of North America to ask her what faith is, and I should not be surprised if she marvels at my question. Before we go, she notices how we admire a large green calabash hanging on a tree in her front yard. The only calabash on the tree, it is about the size and weight of a bowling ball and will be dried and carved to use as a bowl. When she offers it to us, we must accept. It is so generous of her; it would be rude to refuse.

Back on the river, we see a large pod of pink dolphins, so we cut our motor and drift right into the center of it. With a snuffle and snort, the dolphins breathe through blowholes as they surface. What a range of pinks—some look like erasers, others are luminous or dusky. We are close enough to be able to recognize individuals. I lean over the side of the boat and put my head in the water to listen for the rapid clicks of their sonar. *Whoosh! Whew!* they blow as they surface. In pairs and threes they gallop through the river. When the rain starts, we head for shore and climb up a bank to a house on stilts. Inside there are shards of American culture: a Mickey Mouse towel, a photo of Lassie, six lightbulbs for when the house gets electricity, magically shiny pots and pans (one, with a funnel center, looks like an angel-cake pan). The man who lives there pulls out two long benches, the way one puts an extra leaf in the table when company arrives, and invites us to sit. It is simply assumed that we are welcome and may hang up our hammocks in his house if we wish to.

Instead, when the rain stops, we stroll through his backyard and see a mother sloth cradling her baby up in a tree. About once a week, the sloth climbs down the tree, digs a pit, and defecates into it. This exposes the sloth to predators, but by putting its feces at the base of the tree, not dropping them at random, it invests in the future of its home. Algae live in its fur, which gives it a greenish tint. Moths live there too, as well as beetles and ticks. For long minutes, I stand and watch the mother sloth, who is completely immobile until, struck by a ravishing thought, she gently lifts her head.

When the other Zodiacs have joined up with ours, Iain leads us through the rain forest he knows so well. There is much to see: the pau roxo (*Peltogyne*) tree from whose deep purple wood beautiful bowls are made; the lyre-shaped leaf of *Dioscorea,* a vine used as raw material for birth-control medicine because it mimics estrogen; a young kapok tree covered in sharp gooseflesh spines so that rodents can't climb or woodpeckers peck. At first, it seems such a tree must have bounty overflowing that it needs to protect, but perhaps not—there were Renaissance fortress cities supremely well protected, but not because they contained more treasures than other towns. The botanists test trees by making a small slash, looking for latex, noticing the smell, the stigmata of the cambium, a certain readable oozing. As Iain makes a tiny slash in the bark of a strangler fig, white latex tears well up. How old is that tree? I wonder. It is hard to tell the age of a jungle tree because they don't lay down one ring a year. In areas that flood, like this one, many trees have flying buttresses and sprawling, shallow root systems to clutch at the ground. This is not a temperate forest, where sunlight is plentiful, the loam thick and rich, and predictable trees have predictable needs.

As we float down the river, we occasionally smell smoke in the air. Though we are miles away from the sites, we are smelling the devastation of the rain forest, smelling the burning of huge tracts of forest. If the destruction continues at its current pace, all of the rain forest will disappear forever in about forty years. Mining projects, rubber plantations, massive ill-fated cattle-growing projects, hydroelectric dams, highways, and an attempt to burn and dominate the land just because it is frontier and human beings can't abide an unowned space—all have contributed to the destruction of entire ecosystems. Species are going extinct in the rain forest that have not even been named yet. As Iain points out, "We are probably the last generation to have the opportunity to conserve the species of the Amazon forest. . . . Today we stand at the brink of disaster in Amazonia . . . a mass extinction of species—one even greater than when the world lost its dinosaurs."

As the day fades, we return to our Zodiacs and start back down the river, which smells different in the evening than in the morning. In the morning, the oxygen is low and the air lightly perfumed. But in the evening, the air sizzles with oxygen and smells of sedge and damp amber. Pink auroras gush across the sky as darkness falls. With a lantern aimed low at the shore, we search for the eyes of caymans, Amazonian relatives of alligators. To get their attention, we make a mating or juvenile distress call, a syncopated grunting: *Uh! Uh! Uh!* Then we float quietly and wait. To see nature you must be willing to cut the motor and drift, to follow wherever the current leads. But this is tough for goal-oriented people. Some people in my boat chat compulsively, polluting the silent grandeur of the forest. At first I thought they were ignoring the wild, rich sounds of bird, leaf-fall, river, animal, and the august silence, but in time I began to think that it might be the opposite. Talk makes such small shapes in the teeming wilderness of Nature, small shapes in the formless clamor of the universe, but they are shapes for those who need them. They are planks to the shore. "Sshh. Listen," someone says gently, and everyone quiets down for a few minutes, letting the sounds of night wash over them. The steady beat of a frog sounds like someone rubbing a taut balloon. *Corrusha,* a bird called *coruja* calls, a samba in the word. The shore flashes with fireflies, and then a click beetle with two headlights flies over the boat. Our flashlight is reflected in the small revolving campfires of an owl's eyes. At night, there are many mysterious, coal-burning eyes. The reason they seem to shine so eerily is that just behind the retina of nocturnal animals there is a reflective membrane called the tapetum, which helps these creatures see in the dark. Light bounces off of its shiny surface. These live, burning embers in the forest remind us that we are burning, too, from the distant chaos of the sun. An osprey catches a fish and then tilts its beak up so it will be more streamlined when it flies. Cormorants feed near the shore; each has a sort of mousetrap in its throat, the better to stalk fish underwater. Terns swoop in front of us, gliding, then diving in an accelerated stall, careening up into a chandelle, an aerobatic half-loop that ends with the tern rolling over on one shoulder, gaining speed, climbing, and diving again in a bout of aerial sighing and swooning. Bony-tongued fish, *aruaná,* jump to feed. Caboclo fishermen still ply the water in bark canoes, which they steer from the front. Their black paddles are exclamation points dipping into the river.

Fifteen yellow butterflies dogfight and gambol in the green, sedgelike grass of the shore. An Amazon dove whistles. Then a fork strikes a crystal goblet, as if someone were earnestly calling the jungle to order. A flock of parakeets sounds like wet rope twisting into a chirpy screech. Toucans yap like distant dogs. Here and there a low, shallow bark canoe sits on the shore, awaiting its paddler, on business somewhere in the forest. A hawk with bright yellow feet and beak perches on a dead tree branch. Water plashes down a bank from an oxbow lake nearby. When a Brazil nut tree loses two leaves, they fall gently and hit the ground with a hollow clatter. *Wheee!,* a hawk calls like a child with a kazoo. *Wheee!* Soon the rest of the kindergarten band joins in with sandblocks, bottles, tin pans, bells, as different birds take over and the crickets begin to throb and itch with song. An Amazon bird related to the chicken makes a quaking buzz. A trogon calls, *You! You!* We float past a hematanthus tree with bold white flowers, whose alkaloids are used in heart medicine. Tinkling wind chimes fill the air; then comes a howling trill. A spring door slapping and creaking on its frame is a frog.

The new moon makes a slender white canoe above the darkening trees. Bats scout overhead. Iain, knowing of my fondness for bats, tells me that once he saw a bat-eating fish that leaped out of the water, grabbed a bat, and dragged it under. Now the bottle band includes yowling and banshee moans. A white planet, southeast of the moon, floats low over the forest like a shard of ice. In the surging darkness, lights bloom on the river: a single yellow lightbulb from a house; the whiter light of a Zodiac's lantern; the distant flash of a camera where Mo and others are fishing; the twittering greenish-yellow light of fireflies, our ship lying at anchor downstream, lit like a miracle play. In my cabin, deliciously exhausted from the sheer sensory whelm of the day and eager for the days to come, I brew a pot of *casca preciosa* and sip its sweet scented tonic as the ship rocks gently on the ancient river. Then I fall into the well of sleep. For once, dream is the same as the waking world: there I again snorkel in the river by moonlight, hear the muttering of monkeys, and follow a trail of leaf-cutter ants hauling home their small burdens along corridors of scent.

SHORT-TAILED
ALBATROSSES

Coming, going, the waterfowl
Leaves not a trace,
Nor does it need a guide.

— Dōgen (a Japanese Zen master)

This world of ours,
To what shall I compare it?
To the white wake of a boat
That rows away in the early dawn.

— Shami Mansei

The first time I heard the word "Torishima" I was on a ship in the Antarctic, cruising through a garden of sparkling ice, bound for the bird-clotted cliffs of South Georgia. Peter, a painter and ornithologist, was delivering one of his ebullient lectures on albatrosses, his favorite seabirds, some species of which we would soon be climbing tussock-covered hills to view. A short, fair-haired man in his early forties, with a carefully trimmed mustache and beard and the wiry build of a rock climber (seabirds often nest on cliffs), Peter began in a whisper, with the sincerity of someone accidentally overheard at his devotions:

"The open ocean is to birds what space is to mankind—the last great frontier. For birds it poses the harshest, most unyielding environment on the face of the planet, an environment that covers nearly two thirds of the world's surface. Yet it is possible even thousands of miles from land to go to the rails of a ship, look seaward, and see birds. But these are not ordinary birds; these are seabirds. Out of all the world's seabirds, there is one group that is a cut above the rest, one group that is peerless, one group that fills me with awe. They are the most pristine life-form. Those gentle giants are albatrosses. Their kingdom is not one of hillsides, forests, or meadows but is an ever-changing seascape of blue, green, and white, whose moods are unpredictable. Over these vast tracts, albatrosses eke out a precarious and itinerant life. They are the ocean's nomads."

In a British accent lightly tempered by his encounters with a variety of cultures during many years at sea, Peter continued, with the heightened emotion of a painter describing his favorite model. Large, porcelainlike, and stately, albatrosses are among the most beautiful birds. He told us that he had seen every species of alba-

tross in the world except one—the loveliest and most startling—
the short-tailed albatross, a nearly extinct bird with a tragic history, which breeds on only one small, remote, storm-tossed
Japanese island dominated by an active volcano. He had been trying to get there for ten years; at one point, he managed to sail to
within two hundred miles of Torishima, but weather and circumstance prevented him from landing. "Torishima." He pronounced
the island's name with his eyes closed, letting the word pour like a
fresh breeze through the doldrums of his mouth. "To-ri-shima," he
said again, with deep reverence and longing. Slides of albatrosses
appeared in the darkness, as magically as drawings in the caves at
Altamira. As the island's name drifted across the room like an
incantation, I thought of life's wonderful mosaic, how miraculous
and subtle the world's creatures are, and how treacherous human
beings can be to the animals we share the planet with.

The short-tailed albatross once clouded the skies from Japan to
California. It was the most abundant albatross in the North Pacific
and the primary source of nonmammalian protein in the diets of
Aleuts, Inuits, and other North American Indians all the way from
the Aleutians to Baja California. In barely a hundred years, plume
hunters slaughtered almost every single one of them. In a seventeen-
year period alone, five million were killed to stuff mattresses and
quilts. When the U.S. Fish and Wildlife Service surveyed fifteen
thousand square kilometers of the Bering Sea between 1975 and
1982, they found only one short-tailed albatross. The entire
world's population of short-tailed albatrosses had dropped to
approximately ten birds; they had probably come closer to extinction than any other animal on earth. Those that survived did so
only because they found a hiding place on Torishima that was vir-
tually inaccessible to humans. In 1962 the Japanese government
declared those rare, short-tailed albatrosses a national monument—not the island they inhabit but the birds themselves. Now,
about four hundred of them remain: there are about two hundred
nesting on Torishima and two hundred immature birds at sea.
Although the species has rallied dramatically, it is hanging on to
existence by a thread; indeed, despite conservation efforts, it may
become extinct in our lifetime. What could be more important

than to behold these seabirds, to celebrate their beauty and uniqueness? I knew I would have to go to Torishima. Peter and I began planning our trip that evening.

Torishima ("bird island") lies five hundred eighty kilometers south of Tokyo, far from any other land, out in the storm-scoured Pacific. Visiting the island would mean getting special permission, since it has been declared off-limits by the Japanese government, in part to protect the birds, but also because it is an active volcano; an eruption in 1902 killed all 125 of the island's last remaining settlers. Our best hope, we decided, was to join forces with Hiroshi Hasegawa, an extraordinary Japanese ornithologist, who has devoted his life to saving the short-tailed albatross and single-handedly brought their plight to the attention of his government. We would have to go in typhoon season, when the birds were nesting. Apparently, the winds pick up savagely from the northwest in typhoon season, and the only break in the island's stone jaws is one small cove in the northwest corner. There is no beach on Torishima, only volcanic cliffs and sharp black boulders of frozen lava, against which a boat could be tossed and shattered, so we might have to swim ashore, braving sharks and jellyfish. Then we would have to climb the volcano.

Sitting in the lounge of the ship, as it dipped into the long steep swells of the Antarctic sea, Peter and I grinned. It was irresistible. After all, it was his last albatross. For me, it would be a great quest in search of what is rare and beautiful and nearly extinct.

Ten months and much three-person planning later, we fly to Tokyo to meet Hiroshi, who by now has become an epistolary friend. After going through Immigration at Tokyo's International Airport and listing our final destination in Japan as "Torishima meteorological station (abandoned)," we claim luggage and pass through smoky glass doors into the main terminal. The first people we see are a slender Japanese man in his early forties, accompanied by a younger man and woman—Hiroshi and his two graduate students, who swoop down on us like benign falcons, introduce themselves first in the Japanese style, with bows, and then Western style, with handshakes. Peter and Hiroshi look at each other and grin; slender and athletic, with mustaches and beards trimmed identically, they look like Eastern and Western versions of the same species.

"Birders are the same the world over," Peter says, laughing, as we hoist our heavy knapsacks and cases. "We already know a great deal about each other."

One of the things he knows is that birders believe wholeheartedly in the tonic value of ritual, ceremony, and celebration. On the eve of the quest, a special banquet has been planned. As encumbered as an Everest expedition, the five of us set out by bus and two subways, heading across town to the stop for Toho University, where Hiroshi teaches. Climbing out of the tunnels, we enter a world of narrow streets where houses and stores fit together like pieces of a parquet floor that sprawls up as well as along. Night is falling, and hundreds of colored neon lights throb from pachinko parlors, restaurants, and shops. Our travel-weary eyes stretch wide open, to swallow all the strange new shapes, patterns, and changing colors. It is like walking through the branches of a heavily ornamented Christmas tree. In ten minutes, we arrive at a restaurant decorated with photos of sumo wrestlers. A woman with round, smiling cheeks, eyeshadow the color of wisteria, and a bright red mouth drawn smaller than its natural outline greets us at the door, and is obviously pleased to see Hiroshi.

Bowing slightly, she says to us, "Dozo" ("Please"), and sweeps a hand forward in the universal gesture of *Won't you enter*. We slip out of our shoes and leave them at the door among many other pairs perched on the bamboo matting like so many nesting grouse, and follow Hiroshi to a low table in a far corner, where thin pillows have been arranged on the floor.

Peter and I exchange a what-do-you-think-we-should-do-now look and observe our hosts. When the three sit down on their heels, hands resting on their thighs, we do the same. This is the traditional style of sitting, but some of the young Japanese around the room seem to be lounging, American style, one blue-jean-clad knee bent, the other leg stretched out at an angle. Healthier and longer-legged, the new generation of teenagers sometimes finds the traditional style too confining both physically and mentally.

The owner of this small family restaurant is the widow of a well-known sumo wrestler. Hence the decor—calendars of wrestling championships, photographs of wrestlers in action, trophies, and wrestling belts. The menu also favors dishes preferred by sumo wrestlers, but a waitress places in front of each of us a gondola-shaped dish containing three sushi delicacies—a large, thick, chewy sea snail; a pile of ropy white cod's testicles; and a fried squid. Peter and I look at each other, then at Hiroshi, whose eyes are burning with mischief.

"Looks good, doesn't it, Peter?" I say, rubbing my hands together. "Can't wait to try it. Never seen a snail as big as that, have you? Looks like a small palomino."

"No, I can't say I have. And it's amazing the way they have it arranged—as if it's running."

"And the head is so interesting."

"Yes," he says slowly.

I lift the snail in my chopsticks, thinking for a moment that it lacks only a belt around its waist to be a sumo snail, and pop it into my mouth, chew its sweet rubbery mass many times, and smile approvingly to Hiroshi. Then I start in on the creamy, warm cod's testicles.

While we talk of local land birds, a new species of albatross (the "Amsterdam"), which was recently discovered, and how the short-tails are faring, Hiroshi gives Peter chopstick lessons. Fumbling at first, Peter soon lifts the chopsticks to his mouth like a bill and moves the bottom one as an albatross would its lower bill. Hiroshi laughs and does the same, and before long the two of them refine the movement and begin quietly clacking. It is a very esoteric ornithological pantomime, which greatly amuses our hostess, who arrives to light a hot plate in the center of the table. This she tops with a big bowl of *chanko nabe*, a stew of tofu, chicken, vegetables, and indigestible white noodles ("for cleaning out the body"). This is a lighter version of the typical sumo wrestler's diet, sumo nouvelle cuisine as it were. If we were in training, we would get up early, eat lightly, work, and devour our heavy, fatty meal late at night before going to sleep to ensure that our weight reached the three or four hundred pounds a sumo needs to be in top fighting shape. After a few minutes of sitting on our cramped feet, in the Japanese style, we resort to crossing our legs. Hiroshi's English, though halting at times, is surprisingly good. Neither Peter nor I speak any Japanese at all. But the men share a common language of birds and soon are comparing notes in pantomime and in Latin.

"Kampai!" Hiroshi toasts, lifting his glass of beer.

"To Torishima, and the albatrosses," Peter offers.

"Ahodori," Hiroshi corrects him, using the Japanese word for albatross. "It means 'fool bird,' " he says, writing the word down in Japanese, first in the sophisticated hiragana style, then in the simpler glyphs of katakana Japanese—the same bird in an alternate plumage of characters.

"Why are they always thought to be fool birds?" I ask him. Gooneybirds they're sometimes called in English.

Stroking one hand lightly down his beard, he says, "I think perhaps because of how they sometimes look when they land." He makes a tumbling motion with his hands in the air. "But maybe also because they were fools not to fly away when humans came with . . ." He holds an invisible baseball bat in his two hands. "The men murdered one ahodori, another, and another, and the rest of the birds didn't understand what was happening, they didn't fly away. Their killers thought: What fools these birds are, they're so easy to kill."

A bird of such gentleness and beauty was doubly prized by feather hunters, whose trade probably began casually—fishermen gathering feathers at bird colonies on islands they visited. But toward the end of the last century, when Japan began conducting a lot of overseas trade, feathers became all the rage in Europe and the United States. An albatross has between fourteen thousand and sixteen thousand feathers, most of which are small, soft, and downy. There are only ten large feathers per wing, twenty large wing feathers for the whole bird, and as many as twelve tail feathers. So, out of something like fourteen thousand feathers, only a handful could be harvested as quills for pens, or for hats. But the rest made soft, warm stuffing for mattresses and pillows. During a typical year around the turn of the century, Japan exported 380,000 kilograms of feathers, and the trade declined only when the country started to run out of birds.

With a buoyancy I quickly come to prize, Hiroshi lifts his glass of beer and stalwartly offers the expedition toast: "Ahodori! Kampai!"

After dinner, we carry our suitcases through the winding streets toward the Toho University campus. In the shadow of a building, a drunken huddle of college students sway with their arms around one another's shoulders, singing songs into the night. Penguins in the Antarctic huddle this way to keep warm (the French say they are "making a turtle"), and it is the same with chummy fraternity boys the world over. The sight reminds me that we are actually in Tokyo's version of Collegetown. Soon the sumo restaurant's owner catches up with us on her bicycle—we have left behind a birding pamphlet by accident; she thought we might need it. Many bowed heads and renewed thanks. Catty-corner from the campus, we pause at a restaurant, where Hiroshi talks with the owner.

"Tomorrow morning, she will open at eight and give you breakfast," he tells us. "She will expect you."

Then we cross the road, Hiroshi checks us in with the campus guards at the main gate, and we walk past a small flower garden to a building that has university guestrooms on the third floor. At the end of the hall, we find a toilet, a refrigerator, a deep Japanese bathtub, and vending machines offering toothpaste and shaving supplies. We have traveled thirty hours and crossed the dateline, but we are too giddy and excited to sleep. There is still time to watch historic films of Torishima, from Hiroshi's library of albatross books, films, and records (many folksingers and rock groups have sung about albatrosses). So Hiroshi guides us to his office in a nearby building. Venus shines low and bright overhead, like a searchlight that has caught us in its beam. We seem to have fallen through a crack in our culture into a world in which everything is strange and new, and we don't know what sight to expect beyond the next lamppost.

As we climb the stairs to Hiroshi's office, we see photographs of albatrosses on the walls. A light at the end of the corridor welcomes us into a room overflowing with books, wildlife posters, and more photographs of albatrosses, including a large banner on which an almost life-sized adult albatross angles across the sky with wings spread, and Hiroshi's pièce de résistance, a framed close-up of a fluffy, potbellied, short-tailed albatross chick. We sit down on benches around a wooden table. Three graduate students arrive; one brings out a bottle of white wine, another cuts up some fruit, and we all sit down to watch films of albatrosses. The first is an old black-and-white film showing the large flocks of birds that once blanketed the island and pleated the cliffs with white. Japanese observers said that bird-encrusted Torishima looked like an ice volcano, bubbling white. So many albatrosses filled the skies that a constant snowstorm seemed to be traveling around the island. Offshore, the waves appeared permanently white-capped, so large and dense were the rafts of these magnificent birds. Next, in sharp contrast, a more recent color film shows us the few birds that are left, and we shake our heads in disbelief. How could this have happened so fast? The film includes a brief glimpse of the short-tail's extravagant courtship dance. When he sees it, Peter explodes with excitement and bends forward for a closer look.

"They stand on their toes! Oh, and look at that—scapular touch, head wagging, *castanets*!" He lifts his tightly clenched fists in the air and shakes the electricity from them.

Mutually besotted, a courting pair throw their heads skyward again, flap their huge wings, and begin clacking their bills like flamenco dancers gone berserk—castanets. My heart starts to pound. Even on film they are breathtakingly beautiful, with their egg-yolk-yellow crowns. Their quivering bills are pink, with what looks like blue lipstick drawn right at the tip and inside the mouth, and a thin black stripe outlines the base of the bill. Otherwise, the older birds are mainly white. But some immature birds are chocolate-brown, daubed with white epaulets. Leaning forward on the table, crippled by fatigue, we stare in amazement at the small screen, which cannot contain so large a bird, at the two-dimensional sizzle of electrons, which cannot depict the drama that awaits us, and we are saturated with excitement. When the films end, we make our final travel plans with Hiroshi, toast the albatrosses one last time with an uplifted glass and an "Ahodori! Kampai!," and return to our rooms to sleep.

Early the next morning, two graduate students find us having Japanese breakfast at the local restaurant, where, to our delight, we see Hiroshi's photographs of a short-tailed albatross chick hanging on the wall like the familiar portrait of a royal heir. They hurry us downstairs, where Hiroshi is waiting with our luggage. He motions to his watch; there are many miles to cover today, and we must hurry.

With our large knapsacks we look like turtles of an exotic species, carrying our homes with us, but such carapaces make it easy for us to spot one another among the city's tight crowds. One bus, two trains, one monorail, and one airplane ride later we land on Hachijojima, a small volcanic island below the seven islands of Izu, which dot the ocean south of Tokyo like the pearls in a necklace whose clasp has broken. Hachijojima's ten thousand inhabitants are mainly fishermen and their families. Sometimes people fly down from Tokyo to go game fishing, or to take a rest cure at the hot springs. There are no Westerners. The trees chime with flocks of singing bulbuls, clouds surge at night and snag on the peaks of the volcano, and the ocean blows up a fine mist at dawn. Because Hachijojima has the last airport in the islands, travelers heading for even more remote locales begin their far-flung travels from its docks. There is always a place such as this, a crossroads between the familiar and the unknown, a caravanserai in the desert, a Marrakech. In the United States in the nineteenth century it was Mark Twain's St. Louis, where people stopped to outfit themselves before crossing the Mississippi and entering the wild and unruly lands to the west. "Outlanders" such farouche travelers were called, and their ways were dubbed "outlandish." Hachijojima is a smaller crossroads and lacks the con men, hucksters, and desperadoes. It is a last handhold before one wades out into the plunging Pacific. It is a place for the quiet severing of ties to anything like culture. Culture is what people invent when they have lost nature. And there is nothing more certain or powerful on Hachijojima than the wrath of the wind and water, whose compound decree must be deciphered every day from wisdom and weather maps.

On Hachijojima, we stay at a small guesthouse owned by a couple who have become Hiroshi's friends over the years—Eke-san and Toma-san—who meet us at the airport with their van. Toma-san owns a fishing boat and guides game fishermen around the island on sporting odysseys, and he also owns woodlands on the island. Hibiscus and bird-of-paradise spill from the roadway as we drive into a nearby fishing village and up a narrow alleyway to their house near the docks. Leaving our shoes at the door, we abandon the dirt of the outside world and slip into waiting sandals. Even the dust of the world is rich and beautiful in Japanese life, but it belongs outside.

"Dozo," Eke-san says, motioning to a low table in a room dominated by two such tables and a TV set in one corner. We sit down on the floor beside a table, slip our feet under the black-and-white quilted skirt hanging from it, and discover a hivelike warmth underneath. An electric heater attached to the underside of the table showers everyone's legs with a toasty glow. This main room is rectangular and has sliding doors at either side—one set leading into the hallway, the other into the kitchen and backyard. A fitted pink rug runs the length of the floor; there are also two small throw rugs—one with owls, which you step on when you come in from the hallway, one with ducks, where you enter from the kitchen. A cabinet at the far end of the room holds a framed copy of Hiroshi's photograph of the short-tailed albatross chick, which we are starting to regard as our own cabalistic sign. Next to it stands a brass clock, held aloft by two flying cranes (the Japanese symbol of longevity). A wooden plaque with the family's emblem, a sword and a flower, leans on the other side of the cabinet. Ten calligraphy panels stretch above the doors to the hallway.

Eke-san sits down on her knees beside us, bows with her hands on her thighs. A woman of fifty-seven with short, swept-back, dark hair, she smiles modestly and graciously and offers us coffee. Hiroshi turns on the TV to check the local weather, and we scrutinize the weather maps. A northwest wind and a typhoon are heading west through the region. We look carefully at the isobars and discuss the approaching systems. A tight swirl of lines, lying close together and changing direction, signals a typhoon. To seafarers, the pattern is clear as a fingerprint. Three typhoons have passed close to Torishima this year, washing away the soil. As Hiroshi counts the systems, he tucks his fingers in one by one; Peter counts them, too, but bends his fingers outward. We may be spared, but the weather is always dicey in this season, so we decide to wait for the next report.

Soon lunch is served, and lacquered boxes appear with edible mysteries inside. Many new vegetables and fruits and seafood are set in front of us, nameless and piquant, which we eat with a mixture of hunger and curiosity. A large electric hamper of rice stands beside a thermos of hot water near the table. Eke-san smiles at our huge appetites. Birds put on a lot of weight before migration. Some leaf or wood warblers increase their weight by half to make the journey to or from South America. People often do something similar before setting out on an expedition. You don't know when you'll find your next meal.

Bowing our heads slightly, we thank Eke-san in Japanese, saying, "Oishii" ("It tastes good"). Soon we will pay a call on the *sencho* (captain) whose small fishing boat will carry us to Torishima, and we need to buy our provisions. But first we must visit the local government office. Hiroshi returned from his last trip to Torishima with photographs of terrible erosion, and he has persuaded the environmental agency of Japan to send out botanists and soil-management people to see if anything can be done about it.

At an office building in town, a tall man whose name translates as Star Field greets us, and Hiroshi shows him photographs of the Torishima grass, and of the recent erosion in areas his people will be called upon to replant next year. All this commotion must be strange for this local government office. Hachijojima is a small island; Torishima is minute and so out of the way, not just off the beaten track but eruptive, wild, and off-limits. Now, suddenly, the world is coming to Torishima, with video cameras and scientists, as an object lesson in how to pull a species back from the brink of extinction. Hiroshi hopes these botanists and soil specialists will be able to halt the erosion, which is obliterating precious nesting sites. A lot of the island's vegetation has been buried by lava, and in those areas vegetation struggles to insinuate its roots through fresh ash.

A secretary serves us green tea in blue-and-white cups decorated with fans. Light and spinachy, the green tea revives us. Hiroshi hangs his brown corduroy cap from his knee. Two large white scars stretch across the top of his left hand—the stigmata of his trade. He received these gashes handling albatross chicks, whose sharp bills are designed to nab a squid in one blow; by comparison, a hand makes a slow target.

Looking at a photograph of a barren hillside, I see where ash has been blown as if by a dust storm. Plant roots need a mat system so they can bind the loose ash together. And albatrosses need vegetation to build their nests. They dig a shallow scrape in the ground and pull sand and grass together. It's not enough to give a bird an island; you have to give it the right vegetation, too, so that it can cradle its egg. A couple of years ago, as an experiment, Hiroshi planted eulalia on a small area of the island. There was an immediate increase in the number of albatrosses that were hatched. Now he urgently hopes to replace the rest of the island's lost vegetation. He will be asking the botanists to plant in June, the rainy season, with a view to having the nesting area ready for the birds next October.

Ten of these men will be meeting us on the island, and so they discuss supplies and equipment with Hiroshi. When we take our leave of them, we go to a bakery, a grocery store, and a drinks store. If we get weathered in on Torishima, we'll be glad of the extra provisions. Throughout the town we find flagstone sidewalks made of lava honeycombed with air pockets, which is soft and easy to cut. Such beautiful sidewalks are not there for tourists, who come infrequently to Hachijojima. Every day is a special occasion, they seem to say; what touches one's daily life should please the senses. Yellow chrysanthemums, white star flowers, and bromeliads cascade from the steep rock walls that line the winding streets. Some walls are studded with large, sharp stones, hurled by the volcano, which sank into the ash. Standing outside one of the shops, we watch the fishing boats along the wharf as Hiroshi runs down his list. Slightly bowlegged, Hiroshi wears a blue bandanna tucked into the back pocket of his jeans, a blue-and-black-checked shirt, and his brown corduroy cap from the U.S. Fish and Wildlife Service, which he got on a recent trip to Alaska. All the supplies have been purchased. He sighs easily at last. A cormorant perches on a wooden stanchion and we lift our binoculars to our eyes as it arches its wings into a Prussian cross. In China, a fisherman will put a tight ring around the neck of a leashed cormorant (so that it can't swallow what it catches) and have it fish for him from his junk. Unlike other fishing birds, it is not waterproof; otherwise it would not be able to dive so well. Here, in freedom, the bird spreads its wings to dry them in the sun.

"Our first trip to Torishima—very soon now," Peter says, anticipation bubbling across his suntanned face.

"I have been there thirty-seven times," Hiroshi says, "and I am still as excited as you are."

"You've been there more than anyone else on earth, anyone in history," Peter says, letting his binoculars drop to his chest. "And you've been such a good protector of the birds. When you arrive, the albatrosses should line up, rock forward on their feet, and bow." He rocks onto his toes, angles his arms out to his side, and does a stooping half-bow. Hiroshi picks up another part of the courting dance and arches his chest out and arms back. I add yet another gesture by kissing my left shoulder, then my right, with bent arms out to my sides. I do not know what passersby make of this scene, but fishermen on small volcanic islands in the South Pacific are surely used to all manner of strange birds. And the castaneting and whinnying we three do next probably doesn't surprise them much either.

Walking down along the wharf to the fish-packing stalls, we watch the boats unload their catch. In the failing light, only the boat decks shine brightly as men in blue suits and white terrycloth headbands sort mackerel, tuna, and jumbo sardines, tossing them like bars of pure silver into waiting baskets. Hiroshi knows most of these men by sight and salutation. A friend of his lifts a large rainbow by its gills and holds it up with the Would-you-look-at-the-size-of-this-honey expression shared by fishermen the world over; Hiroshi grins appreciatively. Setting the rainbow in a basket, the man gives Hiroshi three large sardines to take home to Eke-san. Oily fish such as these are eaten locally because they deteriorate quickly. The other, white-fleshed fish will be packed in ice and shipped to Tokyo. Thanking the fisherman and wishing him a good season, we head back up the hill, since it's nearly time for dinner.

At home, we find Eke-san arranging flowers. In one room, there is a small display of wildflowers—purple thistles, bittersweet, grasses, and leaves in a black lacquer dish; the water in the dish is as important as the leaves lying in it or the space between the branches or the sky hanging above. There is something robustly damp and feminine about the arrangement, which folds into itself over and over. In another room, a decidedly masculine arrangement of bamboo and bird-of-paradise juts skyward. We sit down to eat, tucking our legs under the quilt, warming them at the heater. Eke-san's twenty-one-year-old daughter brings us hot green tea. Tonight there is a fried fish Westerners call leatherjacket (the Japanese, who find such a name unpalatable, call it "leather remove"), along with sushi, tofu, and vegetables, and mandarin oranges for dessert. Conversations in Japanese and English and pantomime brighten the room. But when the weather report comes on TV, talk stops. In a kingdom of fishermen, the weather is emperor. The only other event that halts conversation is sumo wrestling. This is the week of the sumo championships, and we watch the "Hawaiian Volcano," a rippling mass of human lava weighing five hundred pounds and wearing only a thick jockstrap fringed with what look like drape pulls, ooze across the stage.

"Ah, but he has weak ankles," Hiroshi says knowingly. "In this sport, size doesn't always matter. And unlike American wrestling, there aren't weight categories. Big men can wrestle smaller men, and sometimes the smaller man wins because he's faster." He explains that the strategy lies in knowing your talents, your opponent's weaknesses, and what techniques will bridge the two. Somehow it seems perfectly natural that Hiroshi, a man of zest and good humor who appreciates all the forces of Nature, should be passionate about lighter-than-air albatrosses, so gentle and leaflike, as well as about the many-hammed sumo wrestlers.

With elaborate ceremony, and a stylized referee in ancient costume, the combat begins, and ends a few seconds later when the Hawaiian Volcano stumbles on his weak ankles and his haunches rumble to the ground. This has been so thrilling that Toma-san leaps to his feet and, beside himself with excitement, lifts a glass of strong Japanese spirits to the victor: "Kampai!" he says, fist rolled tight and held aloft.

Jet lag, time lag, and fatigue seem not so much to catch up with us as to collide in our brains, and by nine we are yawning. After thanking our hosts, we climb the stairs and wash at a long communal sink in the hallway. Eke-san arrives a moment later and leads Peter to his room, sliding the main door open, and arranging a mattress on the floor.

In my room, I find a mattress on the floor covered by a cherry-red comforter and a white eyelet sheet. Thanking Eke-san with a small bow, I bid her good night and hear her sandals clatter gently down the stairs. It is a bright, airy, square room with two sliding doors at one end. Each door contains twenty thin, opaque paper panes. On the opposite wall, a wide window, covered by two sliding shutters of twenty small panes of paper, glows a wheat color in the moonlight. Grass mats line the floor. At the tops of walls decorated with a design of tall, blue, leafless trees, a carved wooden trellis opens onto the adjoining rooms. In one corner of my room stands a black lacquer clothes tree in the shape of a Chinese rune. In another corner a television set sits on a low table. Otherwise, the room is bare. Overhead, a square carved-glass light fixture, containing three fluorescent bulbs of different sizes nested one into another, offers various settings of light.

Lying on my bed, I listen to the sound of a cricket chirping somewhere behind a panel. The hallway light shines through the paper panes of the door, which glow softly. The wind blows against a shutter, making it grumble. The carved lattice of pine at the top of the wall allows one room to breathe into another, and I can hear the gentle soughing and occasional snores of my fellow travelers. Tonight I need do nothing but sleep. No worries about chores or appointments to keep. Hiroshi has arranged everything. There is something wonderful about this looked-afterness, which returns us to the world of childhood, when life was a bustling fairground, a thick bloom had begun to develop on one's curiosity, everything felt startling fresh, and all of life's arrangements, the petty worries about directions and payments and meals and timetables, were handled by adults. One was left alone with wonder in an astonishing world. By removing all the fret and bother, Hiroshi has returned us to that freedom.

A violent thunderstorm rattles in during the night, and the winds, shifting suddenly, sound like silk kimonos snagging in the trees. At eight-thirty, Peter and Hiroshi and I meet downstairs for a breakfast of miso soup, fresh-cooked salmon, a raw egg, bread, rice, cabbage, and coffee. A red lacquer box in front of each of us contains strips of dried seaweed.

"Well, what do you think, Hiroshi?" I ask, as I wrap a length of seaweed around a ball of rice and raw egg.

"I don't think so," he says, shaking his head. "Do you play golf?" he asks unexpectedly.

"No," I say.

"I was thinking this morning," Hiroshi says, "about golf. In golf, if you get a hole in one under par it is a birdie, two under par is an eagle, but three under par is an albatross."

"How would one get an albatross?" I ask.

"You'd need a long hole—at least a par five—and you'd have to take two strokes . . ."

Hiroshi and I begin to laugh as the same image dawns on us. From Tokyo to Hachijojima is the first stroke. From Hachijojima to Torishima is the second. We are on an invisible fairway. Fate is choosing its irons.

Eke-san takes two vases of orchids and carries them, with bittersweet and a stalk of bird-of-paradise, into a nearby room. A moment later, a bell rings and incense fills the house. When she returns to the kitchen, I follow the incense trail into the room she left and find a large, ornately carved wooden shrine. In the center of the cabinet, a golden Buddha stands with one hand lifted, flanked by a purple-and-pink candle and a brass key on a yellow thread. Eke-san has left five large persimmonlike fruits as an offering, along with two vases of flowers, a glass of water, and some joss sticks. Brown prayer beads lie on a low table. The carvings of the cabinet all depict birds—cranes and azure-winged magpies—winging forever through the soul of the wood.

Returning to the dining room, I learn that the captain has phoned with a dreary sky report. Who knows how long this storm system may blow. So we find ourselves weathered in on Hachijojima, with nothing to do but sift down deeper into its culture and wait for a calm. In this new climate, we sometimes feel as if we are too heavily dressed, and we take off the overcoat of a cherished custom in one spot, leave the sweater of a familiar habit in another. We no longer use Western cutlery, beds, or toilets. We have stopped consulting watches. Peter and I have both begun speaking courtesy words in Japanese, which we have picked up along the way. The only basic courtesy word we have not learned is the word for "No." We have not yet had any need for it. When we are offered food, we accept it gratefully and eat with much relish. When we are offered drink, we accept it, too, and drink heartily. When we are led along a wharf or through a town or into a store or past a shrine, we follow, feasting our eyes on the panorama as it unfolds around us. We automatically fall into the repertoire of bows, which are social currency. Some require only a small tilt of the head; others are deeper—for instance, when one sits at a table, holding it with both hands, and rocking forward and back. Ten months and five days after we first began planning our trip, we still have two days to travel before we get to Torishima. There are more supplies to purchase, the weather maps to consult like the entrails of a giant bird. Ours is a strong sense of pilgrimage, and just as an initiate must take an arduous religious journey to find what is sacred, we will take many unavoidable steps and endure many hardships on our quest. In ancient times, people went on quests to behold a sacred relic or other artifact. The journey was as important as the goal, more important, in fact, because it was meant to anneal the soft metals of the soul. In Japan there is a traditional art of sword forging in which the metal is heated, folded over, hammered, heated, folded over, and hammered again many hundreds of times. With each step, the metal becomes thinner but stronger. So it is with pilgrimages. When we finally arrive at Torishima, we will be sailing in at night and will have to wait until morning to see the birds. And there will be the cliffs to climb. Few people have ever seen the birds; very few were Westerners; no women. Hiroshi does not subject his graduate students to such a trip; it is too dangerous. Although I am going to Torishima for many reasons, I go in part to stand witness. Lifeforms such as these need to be beheld and celebrated. That is my privilege, as an earth ecstatic, but it is also my duty as a member of the species responsible for their destruction.

Seeing a short-tailed albatross has become a burning obsession. In dreams, I have felt the breeze from its huge slow wings, and pressed its soft, doomed breast to my face. For ten months solid, it has lured me like a winged siren, split open my calendar, drenched my imagination, made me tipsy with excitement, flown wild in my dreams.

Peter began his life in a seaman's orphanage, along with a twin brother and a sister, in Brixham, a small fishing village on the south coast of Devon, in the southwest of England.

"It was a wonderful place," he says, as we sit on the floor in the dining room, listening to the rain fall on a metal roof across the street with a sound like that of quietly played snare drums. "People say, 'Isn't that a shame—growing up in an orphanage and all.' But let me tell you, it gave us all a great start. It was a big granite building, with big gables, green paint, and lots of boys—about fifty or sixty boys—and it was wonderful inasmuch as it taught us how to live. Most of the boys ended up going into the Royal or the Merchant Navy straight from the orphanage. Because it was a seaman's home, we were taught all about the sea. We had a library full of sea books. On weekends and evenings we'd go out sailing with whalers, big whalers. You can imagine what that was like for a nine- or ten-year-old. We used to go sailing, hiking across the moors, doing navigational stuff, rock climbing.

"Just beneath us was a cliff full of breeding seabirds, a place called Berry Head. On Saturdays, we often used to explore the place. You know how boys are. They used to let us out and we just ran wild, exploring everywhere and hanging on cliffs. In the winter those cliffs were absolutely deserted—bare, gray rock. Yet come spring, when the wind was blowing with a hint of ice on it, these birds who had been out at sea would come back and start reoccupying their nesting colonies. If you have an artist's eye, you can draw birds, and you suddenly realize that although you have a common bird, the more you look at it, the more you discover that it's an individual. You start to see little differences in each one. And so it was I got used to certain birds that came back, especially common murres and shags, and I knew which birds were the same ones from last year and the year before. Two years when you're a child is a lifetime. So the return of the breeding seabirds was a big thing in my year. I wanted to see who'd survived and how. I guess at that very early age I fell in love with birds."

Peter left school at fifteen, without any qualifications or certificate, but went on to get an art degree from London University. Then he landed a cushy job as an architect. His wife worked in the next building, and they could walk to work. They had a house, cars, paid holidays, and a pension; life was convenient, predictable, and secure.

"But there came a time," Peter says, "when I said to myself, one day I'm going to be sixty and look back and wonder what I did with my life. I will have held down a job and all that sort of stuff, but what did I really do? With that in mind, we just threw everything up—sold the house, sold the two cars, bought a Land Rover—and I convinced my wife to go round the world. We thought it would take four years to visit all the seabird sites of the world. There really wasn't a good, authoritative seabird guide, and I decided to write one. The four years turned into seven years, and we traveled everywhere, getting jobs all over. Most of the jobs were on boats, since that's the best way to be near seabirds. I worked on all sorts of fishing boats and trawlers and research boats. When we got back home, we were destitute, and I had a family to support. So I took a job as a fish filleter. I used to get up at five and go down to the Fish Gate at six and fillet fish until about midday, wash up, go home, get the book out, and start writing and illustrating. I spent four years working eighteen-hour days. I'd often work beyond midnight. It took three years alone to do those sixteen hundred illustrations of seabirds."

When his guide was finally published in 1983, after eleven years of research, he took a job lecturing for a cruise company, whose ships have become his floating villages. Because they tend to go into remote and exotic locales, they allow him to thicken his life with adventure. He has been to the Antarctic dozens of times. Even on standard voyages, there can be surprises.

"I always tell the passengers," Peter says, " 'If you catch any birds on deck, just chuck them into my cabin.' Well, once, it was a long night at the bar, and when I returned there were forty-two birds flying around my cabin!"

Although he is not a "lister" (a birder who keeps a compulsive tally of sightings), he has seen 315 of the 320 species of seabirds. The only ones that remain to be seen are the short-tailed albatross, the Chinese crested tern, the relict gull, Barau's petrel, and the Fiji petrel (which has been sighted only twice in the past ninety-nine years). By disposition and opportunity, he spends seven to nine months each year at sea. When he's home, he works on large paintings, mainly of seabirds. Most of his time he spends as an ornithologist-guide, renowned for his high spirits, banter, appreciation of the opposite sex, and hard drinking, as well as his stubborn refusal to let anything—rocks, glaciers, storms, deserts— stand between him and a bird. Whenever he lands anywhere, he climbs immediately to the highest point. A year ago, on the observation deck of a ship in the Antarctic, when Peter had just gone downstairs, I heard a woman say to her neighbor, "It's amazing the way the ocean becomes a desert when Peter leaves." But a day rarely passes during which he isn't sketching, painting, or envisioning something.

Finally, one morning the day breaks calm and sweet. We pack hurriedly, eat a huge breakfast, and rush down to the wharf, where a tall, thin *sencho* welcomes us aboard his fishing boat. For hours, Hiroshi has been a combination of intense excitement and absolute dread. Indeed, it is a testimony to his devotion to the short-tailed albatross that he feels willing, even joyous, about making this trip time after time, although he knows it will poleax him with a seasickness whose blades are forged in Hell. Mal de mer is a grief he suffers diabolically—always has, and always will. The ghost of seasickness stalks him for days before every trip to Torishima, and, as he knows, November promises colossally high seas. On board the boat, the first thing he does is take a soporific antiseasickness pill and claim his favorite bunk, while Peter and I climb up to the top of the bridge deck and sit on a hatch. Waving good-bye to Eke-san, Toma-san, and a line of well-wishers, we pull slowly away. A reddish-brown sea turtle swims by like a stepping-stone leading us back to a safe harbor. A line of fishing boats appears on the horizon with scoop nets for catching sardines. Soon Hachijojima shrinks away from us, until it becomes a small gem set in the bevel of the ocean. The boat rolls from one side to the other. A blue mast swings against the paler blue sky. Thick golden ropes hang like military braid down to and around a dark green mizzin. Other ropes lie loosely coiled on the deck like sleeping snakes. In one corner of the poop deck, large white plastic jugs of water rattle against their restraints. Narrower at the top, the mast quivers in the wind. On this six-foot sea, the waves run wild and choppy, but there are no large open swells yet. A stretch of puffy white clouds, quilting the horizon, tells us of an island somewhere below them but too distant for us to see. As the swells become stronger, wave spume looks fluorescent white against the glazed blue of the deep sea—colors familiar in Japanese art. Occasionally the boat jolts—like a drawer slammed back into a desk. Then the sea foam becomes hooves of panic horses.

Peter climbs down to the poop deck and stands at the rail, binoculars pressed to his far-ranging eyes. As the boat careens, he puts his hands in his pockets, bends his knees, and remains perpendicular to the horizon as one side of the boat and then the other swings up—he is the moment arm around which the boat rolls. We enter a realm of swarming fishing boats, each white, with a small, vibrant green mizzen sail at the stern.

"We're out of the shade of land now and into the open sea," Peter says cheerfully, as he climbs back up to the top deck. He looks relaxed and happy. The sea is as familiar to him as a motto. "There is a rhythm to the sea," he says, "a rhythm often missing from one's life. The sea obliges you to adopt its rhythm. You haven't any choice. So I sometimes think of the ocean as the heartbeat of the world. If you stand anywhere on any shoreline, even if it's at a lake, and just listen, letting the stillness descend around you, it doesn't matter where you are, there's always a rhythm, a beat. I love being part of that bigger self. The ocean is a living thing . . . it's fragile, it teaches us how vulnerable we are as a species. But for me it's also an escape route; I find it hard to be in one place.

"And then there are the incredible birds. When I see a seabird, sometimes thousands of miles from land, I'm always filled with a kind of a numbness, because I know that if you took any of us five miles from land and threw us overboard, probably none of us would make it to shore. And yet you can take a seabird that has a brain the size of a pea, take it a thousand miles from land, and it will not only survive, it will return to its original nest site." Lifting one of his cameras, he takes a few shots of the fishing boats pegged like pillowcases against the horizon.

A sudden swell catches us, and our boat skids the way a chariot swivels around one wheel. The cobalt-blue waves grow thick with white lather, as if someone had taken a wire whisk to the ocean. The ship's mate raps on the wooden hatch on which we are sitting. He hands up mugs of soup and noodles and two pairs of chopsticks. My stomach is also swirling, but there is nothing like a plunging sea to make your spirits level, nothing like the snort and lather of the waves to fill you with a galloping sense of adventure. Somewhere on the ocean, there is always a sun street leading to the horizon, a path of glittering light. Outbound, we sailed straight down it. By afternoon, the ocean has turned to obsidian, and the sun street stretches to our starboard side.

At three o'clock Peter spots a black-footed albatross to the east, and within seconds it has crossed the horizon behind and to the west of us at about seventy miles an hour, jetting straight up, then planing sideways and zooming down to the sea surface, only to wheel up again. Albatrosses sail in three dimensions. Dynamic soaring, it's called, a phrase clumsy and mechanistic. An albatross can set in motion a flight so perfectly balanced and attuned to the compound marvels of wind and water that it needn't land, or even flap its wings, for hours, for weeks, indeed, for months. Thanks to the reliable sorcery of physics, the wind right above the water blows more slowly than the wind higher up. If an albatross flying over the ocean wishes to go upwind but doesn't want to flap its wings to get there, it starts a long, slow dive toward the surface of the sea, where it enters the slower-moving air. Suppose the bird is flying at twenty miles an hour in a wind of fifty miles an hour. When it flies in the direction the wind is going, it crosses the sea surface at seventy miles an hour. But when it dives down into the barely moving air near the surface, it has a lot of momentum left over, which it can't shed. Finding itself with all this extra speed, it trades some of that seventy miles per hour for altitude, and shoots up even higher than it was before. It is still flying at twenty miles per hour, but at a higher altitude now, and so it turns downwind again, and continues its perpetual motion of swooping and soaring. Because it's crucial to get into the air moving at the lowest velocity, as near as possible to the sea—every fraction of inch counts—albatrosses maneuver deftly, high-wire artists right at the sea surface. Sometimes you can actually see their feathers touch the water. Over the exploding, crazily tossing sea, albatrosses follow every minute fluctuation of the surface with their wing tips. And they have no need to flap. Indeed, an albatross flying six hundred miles will flap less than a sparrow crossing a narrow street. Almost certainly the albatross we are watching has flown from Torishima, and we greet it as a harbinger, following its swooning path until it finally disappears from sight.

Albatrosses often sail right up to a boat, to feast on cooking scraps or to fish in the freshly churned wake, and sailors welcome them. Of all the birds on earth, albatrosses have enchanted people of all countries through the ages. For one thing, they have colossal wingspans of over thirteen feet and can weigh twenty-five pounds. An eagle or a condor is a runt compared with an albatross. Exquisitely colored, they gleam like satin and are serene, gentle, regal. No wonder they appear in the magic and myth of many countries, as Coleridge knew when he turned one loose in his "Rime of the Ancient Mariner," a poem that has done much to shape the albatross's image as a bird of ill omen. Coleridge had never actually seen an albatross. In 1797, when he and Wordsworth went on a walking tour of Somerset, they decided to finance the trip by each one writing a narrative poem. But Coleridge fretted over a subject. Wordsworth, a lover of natural history, who had recently read an explorer's account of sailing through Drake Passage, gave Coleridge the idea for his "Rime." Baudelaire also wrote about this "monarch of the clouds," which he saw as a metaphor for the poet, so often clumsy in the pedestrian world, but only because of his powerful, huge wings. In *Ida*, Gertrude Stein admired the ceremoniousness of albatrosses: "She had once heard that albatrosses which bird She liked the name of always bowed before they did anything." The Maoris of New Zealand carve albatrosses into the bows of their boats to guarantee a peaceful voyage.

Albatrosses do nest, preferring out-of-the-way places, but they spend most of their lives on the wing, wandering the world's oceans. Nomadic, ever-moving, full of the wind's eloquence and swing, they are creatures bound inextricably to the sea. Amazing as it sounds, they can fly for four or five years without ever returning to land. In low winds, they stretch their wings out full like canvas sails. In high winds, they partly fold their wings and hold them in at an angle to decrease the sail area. Rough weather is an albatross's delight. It can even catnap while it flies. Because it has a small wind-speed recorder in its bill, it can doze while its brain goes on autopilot; a sudden gust of wind will send a quick signal to draw the wings in or stretch them out. In fact, an albatross has been known to hit the side of a boat while asleep. But when they do return to land, they use its green stage for all it's worth. Their courtship involves long, elaborate, Oriental-looking dances, full of kissing and caressing and posing like Kabuki dancers, and symphonic mating calls, which echo from the hillsides where they nest. Observers become enchanted with their beauty and their customs. Their Latin names reflect the majesty and romance people have found in them, translating into such marvels as "pale-backed moon goddess."

The first published account using the word "albatross" was a collection of letters by Dr. John Fryer, published in 1698, in which he describes a voyage around the Cape of Good Hope, en route from South Africa to the East Indies. He spelled the word "albetross," as a corruption of the Portuguese word *alcatraz*, which was used for any large seabird (probably from the Arabic *al-ghattas*: white-tailed sea eagle). In 1744, when Sir William Halley made a voyage to South Georgia, he wrote of the albatross as the harbinger of the Cape. Because albatrosses like to feed over shallow water where there are upwellings, a gathering of albatrosses may well be the first sign that land is near. So they became important symbols of hope. To sailors, they symbolized something more mythic. Albatrosses, as noted, are habitual ship followers, and there is nothing eerier than standing on the deck of a ship, looking up, and seeing a bird as large as, say, a wandering albatross, with a wingspread of almost fourteen feet, sailing up to you, floating absolutely motionless on outstretched wings, looking down and cocking its head sideways as though it knew you. Superstitious men claimed that albatrosses were the reincarnated spirits of dead sailors who were searching for their friends. Lighter than air, formed of wind and whitecaps combined, they floated like restless transmigrated souls. Nonetheless, sailors have killed albatrosses and found uses for most of their body parts. The oily vomit was used to waterproof boots, the downy breast feathers to make muffs or capes, the sewn-together skins to make feather rugs. Rendered carcasses produced fertilizer and oil. Sailors fashioned tobacco pouches from the webbing of the feet and pipestems from the hollow wing bones.

Soon the sun slides behind a thick wall of coriander clouds and finds one small hole, where it hangs, a perfect ruby above the horizon, vanishing at last in a shimmying lager of mauve clouds. After sunset, we climb down to the poop deck and crawl into the low-ceilinged cabin, cluttered and dim, which looks like a room that a truculent child has refused to tidy up. Twelve feet long and six feet wide, it is only about three feet high. On a gas hotplate, a green enamel kettle is corralled in stainless steel. Next to it sits a white porcelain rice steamer, under a calendar whose photographs show Japanese fishermen at work. Although this cave is much too small and low to sit up in, all manner of electronic gear is crammed into the space—a VCR, a TV, a weather-fax receiver, navigation screens—and there is even a wooden shrine. Six of us stretch out on blue and green blankets in the hot cabin, which is thick with cigarette and cooking smoke. The *sencho* passes out bowls of rice, yams, fried tofu, eggs, shrimp, and squid. As the others eat heartily, I get violently seasick into my bowl, turning away into a corner as much as possible. With nothing inside to nourish me for over twenty-four hours, I will have to drink a lot of water when I get to Torishima. But soon it feels good to be so empty, so ready to be nourished again. After dinner, the crew chat quietly among themselves in Japanese, and Peter and I speak in English. Our languages flow with such different tempos and inflections that each drifts easily through the open weave of the other. At times I feel that we are time travelers, stepping between the tick and tock of mere chronicity into a world where we live at last by seasonal time.

Arranging his shoulders against the wall, Peter tucks a rolled-up jacket beneath his back and tries to find a place for his legs in the jumble of limbs. The *sencho* passes him a can of beer on whose label a mythical animal prances, half horse, half dragon. In the glow of a single lightbulb, we sit thoughtfully as the tiny fishing boat slides down the ocean's hills of glass. The sea looms dark as the inside of the earth, no matter which way I look across its flat expanse. There is only our one light burning. We are such fragile entities to be adrift on this vast ocean. I am reminded of the sailor's prayer: "Protect me, Lord, for the ocean is so large, and my craft is so small." A hard swell rocks the boat, rolls sleepers into one another, and hurls loose pots and pans from their moorings.

"Typhoon season," I say. "Now I understand why they're called the 'high' seas. But I bet you've met some wonderful folk on them."

Bracing one arm against the ceiling, Peter just keeps from rolling over a sleeping crewmember.

"You know," he says, "ocean people are without doubt some of the brightest, funniest, and in some ways saddest characters that you could ever hope to meet. I think the ocean brings out the best or the worst in people, and there are some hilarious times, and there are times, of course, when you're in peril and so on, but basically speaking, you can have a better time on the ocean than you can ever have on the land. You meet more bizarre people. They have a rhythm of life that is like the ocean. It's rarely placid—it's either blowing hard or blowing incredibly hard. There doesn't seem to be any lull—there is always something going on within their lives, whether they're fishermen or researchers like myself.

"Two of the most colorful characters I ever met were people who lived down at Bluff, on South Island in New Zealand. When we traveled around in our Land Rover, we often had to work illegally, without work permits, and it was a question of my knocking on people's doors and asking for a job. I worked for very low wages, but I hoped to be able to work with seabirds. Money was always a problem. I must have had about two hundred dollars to my name at that stage, and here we were halfway around the world with no jobs, trying to find work in a fishing port. And Bluff is New Zealand's equivalent, say, of Steinbeck's Cannery Row. There were wonderful characters. The language was awful. I've never heard such language in my life. I'd been going around the three bars in Bluff—all of them what I call spit-and-sawdust places—frequented just by fishermen. So I'd been going around for about three weeks, and I knew that I'd been to all of the skippers, and they'd all said no. They could hear that I was English, and of course that was not necessarily a good thing, because I was not a local. But if I've got anything in life it's perseverance. I went into this bar, which I'd gone into many times over the previous weeks, and I saw two people sitting there who had always impressed me, just because of the disparity between them. There was one chap who was smaller than myself but broader, with a great mop of fair hair, and he was George West. The guy with him was as big as George was small. He must have been about six foot five or six foot six, equally as broad as George, with a great mop of black hair. Both were Maoris. The reason that George was fair was that his father was a Russian sealer who had jumped ship and had married the chief's daughter.

"Well, I walked up to them and without being invited sat down next to them. They didn't even look up. I introduced myself. I said, 'Since I last saw you I've tried every damn fishing vessel in the fleet, and I'm not getting anywhere. I'm not getting any work offers whatsoever. Although I don't know crayfishing boats, I have worked on trawlers, I've filleted fish, and I'm pretty handy on a boat. There's no way that I can convince you guys of this, but I'm so confident of my ability that I know that if you just take me out for one voyage, you'll see. Don't even pay me—but at the end of the voyage, if you think I'm worth anything, let's sit down and talk about it.' There was still no response. Big John sort of looked up and took a swig from a glass, which really was a half-pint glass at least a quarter filled with whiskey. They were hard drinkers and hard workers and men of the ocean. And George looked up and he started talking about something completely different. Started talking about the fact that the fish weren't running, and whether they should try farther south, and I realized that I wasn't getting anywhere at all. I looked at the bartender and I asked for a glass, and he came and put a glass down which was equal in size to theirs, and George looked up and he said, 'Do you want a drink?' And I said, 'Sure, I would like a drink, but mostly I would like a job.' George disregarded that remark completely and took hold of the whiskey bottle, which was placed on the table in front of us, and started to pour. Not into my glass, but first into his and then into Big John's glass, and he paused just long enough to at least have considered not giving me a drink, and then he started to pour. He poured as much into my glass as he had into their two glasses. Then he put the bottle down with rather more of a thump than was necessary, and I rather suspected that we were going to have some bravado in store for us. He picked up his glass and he looked straight into the eyes of Big John—and as I got to know George, I found he had a wicked sense of humor—and he said, 'Well, let's hope the next trip is better than the last one.' He raised his glass and in one movement swallowed a quarter of a pint of whiskey, and then put his glass down on the table. Big John took up his glass and, without so much as a word, raised the glass and tossed his head back and the whiskey was gone. There wasn't any exclamation, there wasn't a gulp, it just disappeared, as though he was pouring it down a pipe. My father used to talk in lots of little sayings, and one of his favorites was *When you're with men, act like one.* I was only about twenty-seven years old, but I raised my glass, looked both of them in the eye, and said, 'And I hope that I'm with you.' And I tossed that whiskey back. I have never, ever felt worse in my life than at that point—from embarrassment, from retching. That whiskey hit me and before it was even past my throat my stomach was protesting. It was convulsing, my throat was burning. But I held that glass out, and I could see that they could see that I was shaking. My whole body was shaking, and the glass went down and hit the table and there were tears streaming out of my eyes and I looked both of them in the face, and George looked at Big John with a sideways look and a sheepish grin and he said, 'You know, this bastard is all right. I think we'll take him.' The time was just after five in the evening, and I don't know how long I lasted, but shortly thereafter they took me out and threw me into the back of a pickup as though I was a dead sheep or something, and they drove me out to the campsite, which is where we were living. They knocked on the door of the Land Rover. My wife opened the door and was horrified to see one huge bloke and another man, a dwarf, almost, holding me, who was by this time absolutely unconscious and reeking of whiskey. They threw me in on the floor. George turned to my wife and said, 'Tell that bastard if he sobers up and still wants to go, we're leaving at six in the morning.' And that was the start of two and a half of the most wonderful years of my life.

"It was a wonderful time, being a crayfisherman at Bluff with George and Big John. They used to sit telling stories at the end of every day's fishing. We would be working about eighty or so miles out of Bluff, off the end of Stewart Island, down south in the fifties. It was cold and there was ice on the rigging. You'd have to spread salt on the decks to keep the decks from freezing up. I was the winch man and the cook and the pot baiter. I've always been a reasonably good cook so there was no problem in that, but the other two jobs were very hard, especially handling the winch. We used to work on a crayfishing trawler which was made of quarter-inch steel plate. Must have been about sixty-five to seventy feet long, so it was a fairly big boat. John and George were like chalk and cheese in many ways, but both of them had a very good sense of humor and both of them, I guess because they were Maoris, didn't think in terms of a Christian God. They were people that lived more by natural signs and a natural way of life. And they both had been working, as their families had before them, on those islands. We were in a place called Big Mogey—and if you can imagine a horseshoe-shaped island and the indentation facing to the east and all the weather coming from the west, you'll see that we had a wonderful safe anchorage. We were always working between storms, and some of the days were incredibly rough, and waves would be breaking over us as we were on the deck, and there'd be the odd times when you'd be literally wiped off your feet and smashed against the gunwale. On a couple of occasions Big John would pick me up like a terrier, shake me, put me back down on the deck. He was immensely strong.

"Well, one day we had a warning of bad weather. Now we were always having gales coming through, so people didn't worry about the normal force-ten gale; we worked in that. But we had warnings over the radio that there was a really big storm coming and that everyone should try to get back to port. Port was about eighty miles away and we realized that we really couldn't outrun the storm, so all the boats in the area went down to an island called Pukenai, about eighteen miles to the south. There must have been about

forty boats all running down to Pukenai. But George wasn't going
to run. As he said, his grandfather hadn't been, as he called it, assholed out of Mogey, and his father hadn't been, and sure as hell
George West wasn't going to be assholed out just because there was
a puff of wind coming. So we stayed put. We dropped anchor and
got stern and bow lines out and got everything sort of ready. Then
the storm hit and it was absolutely horrendous, so we sheltered in
a little bay. The island was all around us on three sides, but we had
this window at the back of us, where we could see the storm and
the waves going by, wall after wall of water, fifty feet high, wiping
the island, ripping up trees that had been on that island for eighty
years. As the waves went past, a suction effect started on the back
of the island that was incredible. So we were going up and down
and the albatrosses were hurled past—royal albatrosses, wandering, black-browed, gray-headed, sooty—it was just fantastic. There
were penguins around us, and other birds getting blown all over the
place in the gale. It's really wonderful to see a twelve-foot bird like
an albatross picked up and blown around. This storm blew and
blew and blew for one entire day. As it started going into the second day, it actually got worse. In storms of from force ten onwards,
the water gets lifted up off the surface of the sea. When you look
out, it's almost as though there's a blizzard. Huge waves are coated
in spray and white foam—we call that steaming or smoking. And
when the sea is steaming or smoking, then you know you really are
into something. We stayed there and kept radio contact with the
guys on Pukenai. They were behind a big island, and perfectly safe.
George was telling these people down at Pukenai: 'You chickenshit
little assholes'—I apologize for the language, but this is how he
used to speak—'You're not men. You're supposed to be men of
steel in wooden boats,' he said. 'There's not a man amongst you!' I
knew from the outset that he was openly courting disaster. You
cannot make those sorts of comments and get away with it all the
time. We got through the second day, and it was on the third day
that this storm just sort of settled over the southern end of Stewart
Island. It was howling. Whole trees blew right across the sky, and
all the water was muddy from the soil that had been torn off the
island. It was just incredible. I've never seen a storm like it. We were
trying to have breakfast and suddenly the boat just twitched

slightly to port and George and Big John were up and over the table. And I was left sitting there, thinking, What the hell's going on? Big John, the engine man, cranked up the engine fast, and as he was cranking it I saw George struggling with the fire ax, which was almost as big as George. He was going out the wheelhouse door with this ax, and I was thinking, What on earth is going on? Of course, I ran out after them. The engine kept missing and wouldn't start, and George was on the stern of the boat, swinging the ax, cutting through the two-inch-thick mooring ropes. In four or five hits, he took the second stern line out. It was then that I looked around and saw what had happened. One of the bowlines had broken. Both George and Big John were so finely attuned to the boat and the ocean that they knew there was no way we were going to get that line back on again. George then ran up to the bow—we were facing with the stern pointing out towards the sea—and he ran up to the bow and he waited until the engine fired, and as soon as the engine fired, in one sweep he cut the last rope. And we were washed straight out of that little bay. We had no time to warn the guys at Pukenai that we'd been assholed, as George put it. And as soon as we were out, he got on the radio and made contact. It was about seven or eight in the morning, and of course suddenly everyone was tuning in. The seas were absolutely horrific. It took my breath away. The waves were mountains. Sometimes you can be in waves that are fifty to sixty feet high, but they're long. You might have three hundred yards between them. But these things—it was like being put into a small canyon. The wave crests were only about thirty to fifty yards apart, and they were anything from forty to sixty feet high. The whole sea was smoking. George was radioing, saying, 'We've been assholed.' And to start with everyone was laughing and calling him names, saying, 'So you've been assholed! We told you, you son of a bitch.' And then abruptly there was a change. George said, 'We can only do one thing; we've got to run with the waves to you.' And they knew that was about eighteen miles. Suddenly, instead of all the banter and lampooning that was going on, there was a quiet, a lull, a serious concern. They were saying things like 'Stay in radio contact,' and 'If you get in any sort of difficulty we've got a boat started up and we'll try to come out.' We knew that was impossible, of course. But it was wonderful to be on the bridge and to know that there were about forty ships all tuned in over the radio, listening to our progress. And George gave them one hell of a progress report. He'd be screaming, 'Here's another one of these motherfuckers, it's sixty feet high, it doesn't scare me. You stupid shit. There's no God out there, there's nothing big enough to take my boat. I might have been assholed out of Mogey, but I'm not going down to Davy Jones. I'm not being taken out by Davy Jones.'

"I used to look around when he'd talk like this, and I'll tell you, it would go dark. You'd be standing in the wheelhouse and it would go dark, and you were scared to look back at that huge wave following us, because on a crayfishing trawler most of the equipment was on the front end of the boat and there was only a big platform on the back. If any of that water had actually caught up with us and cascaded down over us, it would have pushed the stern straight under and we would have been sunk. Time after time the waves broke and we would have six feet of water crashing onto the deck. We would be standing in three feet of water in the wheelhouse and George, still at the top of his voice, would be screaming, 'You don't scare me, nothing's going to sink us, we're going to get there. If you think you can do it, try! This ship is better than any wave you care to send. Next one, send me the biggest. Give me your best shot, and I'll show you!' And I was saying, 'George, George, don't you think, don't you think you ought not to tempt . . .' And Big John was just standing there, worried, smoking a cigarette. Then two big waves hit us close together and even George lost his footing, and we all ended up falling, and there was water all around us. I thought we'd sunk. I thought, This is it; get your boots off and start swimming. We were all topsy-turvy, and George was still laughing like hell and saying, 'You bastard, you missed, you missed!' Over the radio, we heard: 'George, what the hell's going on there? Are you afloat? Are you swimming? George, where are you?' And George got hold of the radio and he said, 'Nothing's big enough to sink me. This is quarter-inch steel plate. I built this boat with my own fucking hands, and water is not taking me to Davy Jones!'

"I'll tell you, it took us about three hours to do that eighteen miles. It was awesome. There was a small pass behind Pukenai, and when we came through it everybody was on deck—from a mile out you could hear them cheering. We came in there and we were heroes. We were men in a man's world. The storm petered out that afternoon, but we spent two days drinking and getting absolutely paralytic. We went home after two weeks of fishing, having caught only four and a half pounds of crayfish. Now *that* was a storm."

The *sencho* leans deep into the cabin, whispering "Torishima, Torishima!" and pointing off the stern of the boat. In a rush, Peter and I climb over the sleepers and out onto the deck. The night is iced with stars, stars in a wilderness of stars. The lights of four distant fishing boats twinkle off our port side. Then I begin to see a greater darkness in the night—Torishima bulging up right in front of us. Peter and I look at each other in joy and disbelief. We are here, actually here at Torishima, after so many months. But it is still a mystery. And where are the birds?

"Camp," the *sencho* says, pointing to one side of the island. We follow the line of his hand, which indicates a direction, but no land or safety, only a trail into deep space. Our base camp is invisible, in the foothills of the coming morning. This should not surprise us, being so much like life itself, but it does.

We nod, thank him, and stagger back to the cabin; it is like crawling into a low, floating cattle shed. Peter arranges himself against one wall, and I against the other. We close our eyes and try to sleep. There is no use waking Hiroshi. There is nothing anyone can see or do until daybreak. After a few minutes of silence, a brief, mournful call strikes across the waves.

Peter's eyes flash open; he sits up, whispers excitedly, "Hear that? Short-tailed albatross!" Then he lays his head back down on his fisherman's sweater, against the large clock, below the ornate gold mirror, next to the set of large fuses, and falls asleep, smiling.

At first light, we rise and stumble out onto the deck again; this time we see the black, nugget-shaped island clearly. We have drifted a little in the night, and the *sencho* quickly climbs up and actually stands upon the wheel, steering it with one naked foot. Hiroshi wakes up and joins us with a broad smile. "Torishima!" we cry in unison, arms open wide, like opera singers frozen in the midst of a great aria.

• • •

Making many Zodiac runs, the *sencho* drops us off, with fifty boxes and heavy sacks of food, water, and camera equipment in a steep, boulder-strewn inlet. We wave good-bye to him and turn and face one another as if for the first time. Hiroshi unpacks tall jugs of Chinese tea and orange juice, and we pass them among us, along with sweet rolls. Neither Hiroshi nor I have eaten for twenty-four hours and we are hungry, but this is, implicitly, a token meal, a chance to pause a moment at the island's rim and break bread together.

"Torishima," Peter says quietly, nodding as if in answer to a question.

"Torishima," I say, feeling some of the same cold thrill I felt the first time I looked through a telescope. There was Saturn with its broad sherbety rings and all its radiant moons in tow, exactly where it was supposed to be. A hidden world.

"Torishima," Hiroshi says, with the pride of an innkeeper unlocking a mythic realm.

High above us, on a promontory jutting out from the sharp, twisted tumble of black rocks, stands the small cement garrison that will be our home. Getting there means climbing up fourteen stories of almost vertical rock. The men carry the heavy loads, silently, though their faces groan. Puffing hard, I balance lighter loads on my head, as women do the world over, and carry sacks draped around my body. At an especially awkward point, we work together—Peter tosses boxes up to me, and using that momentum, I toss them higher, to where Hiroshi lifts them higher still. Before long, everyone's hair is slicked down by sweat.

"Friends," Hiroshi says, pointing to a second inlet, not far from the one in which we landed, where the government team of ten men has begun unloading their supplies, too, and climbing like a long caravan of ants up the mountain. Some carry stacked boxes in front of them; others have plastic baskets roped to their backs. We wave to them and haul our first supplies over the last ridge to the garrison. Set back from a patio of rock where the remains of a cannon sits, the building has one doorway and windows no wider than a rifle barrel. In front of it lies a curious heap of neatly arranged lozenges. Long ago, bags of cement became wet, liquefied, and hardened. In time their outer sacks weathered away, leaving this array of stone pillows.

Hiroshi walks inside the building, looks around, picks up a half-decayed rat with a gaping mouth, tosses it outside, says, "Yes, this is home."

Greeting the government team halfway down the mountain, we combine forces and spend the next hour hauling up all the supplies. When some of the men finish, they unpack small amber-colored bottles of a stamina drink and down the tonic in a toss. The cook they've brought with them has already begun preparing rice, as the men see to their knapsacks. Inside the bunker, the sleeping arrangements follow a strict protocol. A low wall of boxes runs down the center of the room.

"You eat away your privacy," Peter says, laughing, as he helps to stack the boxes filled with everything from dried seaweed to tinned squid.

Ropes divide our space from that belonging to the other ten. Hiroshi, Peter, and I will be sleeping in one corner, barricaded by boxes, with me between the two men. This arrangement conveys a clear unspoken message: she's being guarded. We don't expect any trouble. But I am the only woman in a camp in the wilderness with twelve men, and our provisions include alcohol. Best to take extra precautions. As we begin to unpack some of our personal items, Hiroshi presents me with a green sleeveless poncho made of nylon. Light and voluminous, it falls in drapes to the ground, and it has one elasticized hole at the top. He reads the puzzlement on my face.

"To change your clothes," he explains, smiling. "It's what women use in canoes."

I shake my head in amazement. He has thought of everything.

By now, some of the men have set up a low wooden table on the ground in front of the building and rolled up a log at either side, and we all sit down for a quick breakfast of peanut-butter-and-jelly sandwiches, cheese, fish, and rice. Hiroshi hands Peter and me plastic nesting bowls and red enamel mugs. His own mug is black-and-white with a green kingfisher on it and the slogan *We love bird-watching.* After breakfast, the three of us stand near the edge of the cliff, drinking coffee, regarding the opalescent dawn light over the sea; suddenly a dark form appears above us and arcs

across the sky. Peter swings round and cries, "Short-tailed albatross—immature!" Hiroshi and I do a small war dance with him,
and then formally congratulate him.

"Eight thirty-eight A.M." Hiroshi notes, checking his watch.

Peter has seen his ultimate albatross, and he puts one hand to his
chest, where there is a sweet jubilant pain. Joy floods his face. For
ten years, he and Hiroshi have been exchanging letters about his
coming to Torishima; Hiroshi had warned him not to wait a lifetime. And now here he is, standing on a rock outcropping once
occupied and abandoned by feather hunters, a garrison, and a
weather station, seeing his first short-tailed albatross. This one
was immature, in its brown colors. He longs to see the adults with
their golden crowns and their pink bills, and we decide to set off
at once.

As everyone prepares for the hike across the island, we indulge
in small good-luck rituals—retying our shoes, adjusting our helmets, tucking our pants into our socks as protection against scree.
Then thirteen of us set out in a long caravan, climbing behind the
garrison, past the abandoned weather-station barracks, over a
steep meadow of grasses and low, bunchy, yellow chrysanthemums. Below us, skirts of frozen lava ripple toward the coast,
where they once enveloped a whole village. Making our steepest
climb in the early part of the day, we cut across the mountains
more obliquely, walking up a glacier of crushed lava, and over
ground singed with bright yellow sulfur salts and hot black scabs.
By midmorning, we reach the flattest place on the island, at the
base of Sulfur Peak. There a field of lava rocks—missiles ejected
from the volcano—has turned the narrow col into a wind-blown
moonscape of starkest black and white. Moon Desert, Hiroshi
calls it. He points to an emptiness at the end of the col, where the
land drops away and the entrance to the cliffs begins.

"We'll be able to see the albatrosses from there," he says excitedly.

Everyone else rushes on ahead, but Peter and I walk slowly as
before. At last we cannot make the moment wait any longer. The
col opens into an explosion of tall pinnacles and wind-ripped
cliffs, where rock walls spill down through twisted chasms. There
before us stands the fortress of the *ahodori*. Far at the bottom,

down an impassable set of interlocking cliffs, a small flock of brown-and-white birds dot the grass. They look like handkerchiefs someone has dropped onto a lawn. An invisible fist knocks the breath out of me and I sigh out loud. There are so few of them. It is heartbreaking to see the last remaining nesting short-tailed alba-trosses on earth. Over the breeze, we can just make out their whis-tles and whinnies, and their castanets, which sound like hollow wooden pipes hitting one another. The scene throbs with color— the bulging, oxidized orange cliffs, the green grasses below, on which the albatrosses nest, the tan rock face, the golden ochers, the black lava. Through binoculars, I see the yellow crowns of the birds, so close now, but still so inaccessible. Above them, a fanta-sia of albatrosses sails across the sky. Men built a garrison at the other side of the island, but nature built one here that is far stronger—almost impenetrable. Because of this natural fortress, based entirely on the bad temper of rock, the birds have survived the onslaught of humans. Peter stands at the lip of the cliff, one hand lightly pressing his binoculars against his chest, his eyes damp with emotion.

Hiroshi joins us, and we three stand silently and behold the fortress for some minutes. It is utterly astonishing that Hiroshi has been studying the birds in such an impossible locale for the past ten years, that he has managed to bring out news of them and even on rare occasions to take the outside world down below for a closer look. That the birds are increasing in number is a great tes-timony to Hiroshi's work and to the support of the Japanese gov-ernment. It's comforting to think that in a high-speed world, where people sometimes content themselves with shallow efforts, naturalists like Hiroshi are devoting their lives to saving one species. What a rich remembrance, to know that you preserved a miraculous form of life from disappearing forever from the planet.

"Let's go," he says at last, and we set off along the east side of the walls. Hiroshi has marked a large O in white paint on some of the more secure rocks along the way. It is a steep, slippery descent down sheer four-hundred-foot cliffs. When we come to a particu-larly awkward plunge of rocks near the edge, Hiroshi attaches a rope to a rock. Passing the rope behind the waist, and holding one section in the right hand, one section in the left, a strong climber can lean back against the rope and use it to slip and brake his way down without using a harness. I have never climbed with ropes before, but I like the feel of the rope as it slides and rasps through my hands. Leaning back, I try to lower myself slowly, but my foot swivels, and suddenly I skid downhill toward the cliff edge, clinging to the rope. Loose stones clatter below. Everyone freezes. Above me, I see Peter, Hiroshi, and the ten other men transfixed to the rocks, watching me suspended over a four-hundred-foot chasm, all the emotion smashed out of their faces. There is no point in looking down. My mind fills with a single thought: *Don't let go of the rope.* Hanging on with my left hand, I bring my right hand around, find a handhold, and pull myself back up. Once I find my footing, I continue across a rocky bridge and let the rope loose for the next person. Above me, people begin to move normally again. The next climber takes the rope, becomes confused, freezes midway across, and will not go on. Peter climbs down after him, at last coaxing him along. Despite their knapsacks full of photographic and surveying equipment, the rest of the team gradually work their way down the first section of cliff, and then we angle across to a more severe plunge. Here Hiroshi has hammered four pitons into a rock at the top, from which he has hung a rope. Peter and Hiroshi have both been rock climbing for many years, and I understand at once how seductive it can be. At each station along the way, you feel hawklike, perching high in towering freedom to pause and look out over the valley below and the ocean beyond. But I especially like the puzzle of figuring out which rock will make a handhold; what tablet, pyramid, or silo of earth to cling to; on what slender ledge to place my foot. At times, you are violently gripping the bones of the planet, and at others tiptoeing down the shallowest stairway. It is a strange, tentative searching with all of your limbs that unites you, as nothing else could, to the core of the planet, to the violence that forged it, to the thrust and fall of the rock frozen forever in the memory of a mountain. Rocks have veins and faces. And there is the texture of rock—in one moment raspy, spiky, and brutal; in the next gentle, forgiving, and smooth. There are the colors of blood, midnight, and autumn. There is the steep persuasion of gravity, drawing you down its rocky spine. Again I misstep and, holding on to the rope, slide back into a ledge, collect myself, and continue down to where Hiroshi, seeing that I'm all right, leaps into a hill of deep sandy lava and cascades with it clear down to the bottom. Peter does the same, and I follow. Then we scramble up a small dune and suddenly find ourselves staring straight across a plateau at two bustling colonies of short-tailed albatrosses.

Nesting, yawning their wings, romancing, tending their eggs, bickering, they go about their normal ways, only two hundred yards from us, far enough not to be frightened by our presence. Vibrant white, with radiant yellow heads and coral-pink bills tipped in blue, the adults are unbelievably beautiful. A subtle wake of shadow runs behind each dark eye. Glossy, elegant, smooth as wax, they stretch their airy wings and, even while sitting, embrace the wind. The adolescent birds are brown or have mottled plumage of brown and white, some with striking white epaulets. All wear small, discreet colored bands around their legs—a present from Hiroshi so that he can identify them. Each color denotes a different year. A white band, for example, was put on the right leg of each of the forty-seven birds hatched in 1986. The two colonies of birds are separated by a black, swirling drape of lava, which is narrow enough for the birds to walk across. Young birds sometimes take a mate in the other village and settle there. Depending on the wind, a bird may land in the lower village and climb up to the higher one. The older birds (with whiter plumage) prefer to nest in the center of the colonies, the younger birds near the edges. Some are sitting on eggs. Occasionally a bird will stand, rearrange its feather petticoats so that the egg nestles tightly against the warm brood patch, and then, with a twitch or two, settle down deep into its soft haunches again. Two eggs lie outside of nests, which means the chicks within will have died. In a species as rare as this, where every newborn counts, that is a tragic sight.

A particularly lovely female with a bill the sultry coral of a Bahamian sunset opens up her downy wings and preens them gently. Every single feather has a nerve ending she can use. I try to imagine what it would be like if I could put my arm out and twitch each hair separately. A male approaches her, and suddenly she spreads out the white skirts of her wings and curtseys to him. He curtseys back. Then he reaches with his bill and brushes up a few of the feathers on her breast. This drives her wild. She slides her bill down along the side of his and starts delicately kissing the small feathers at the base of it. He does the same to her, and they pull back a few inches and start a crescendo of clacking that sounds like a spoon hitting hollow wood—castanets. They roll their heads together from side to side, as if packing an imaginary snowball. He rocks forward onto his toes, aching toward her, and presses his chest out like a sail in a strong blow; she does the same. Suddenly they toss their heads skyward, stretch their necks long in mutual yearning, quiver and flap and trumpet to high heavens.

Their wild, otherworldly music drifts across the grass, half whinny, half moo, like "the surrealistic lowing of cattle," as Peter describes it. Next they do a "Groucho walk" around each other— a low-down strut with their shoulders hunched—and then they face each other and start to curtsey again. While this erotic minuet continues, dozens of black-footed albatrosses, a darker and less extravagant-looking species nesting nearby, engage in more modest courtship dances of their own, in which they sound like speeding cars screeching around tight curves.

All at once, a white short-tailed albatross sails in off the ocean, flies a wide spiral around the colonies, banks and tilts with fluent grace, and begins what's called reefing. Arching its chest, it pulls the huge sails of its wings in halfway, lets its big feet hang down like a plane's undercarriage, ruffles up its tail feathers as a sort of air brake, and tries to slow down enough to land. Round and round it flies, soaring and reefing, swooping low and funneling high, with an eloquence that leaves us gaping, not quite sure on which pass it will lose flying speed and touch down at last. The sunlight shines through its yellow feet, as if through the paper panes on a sliding door in a Japanese house.

"Kirei," I say, more an exhalation than a word. It is Japanese for "beautiful." And I mean all of it: the heat mirage, like a transparent curtain of shot silk between us and the colonies; the nesting birds, perfect as alabaster statues; the ceremonial square dance of the courting pairs; the incoming bird whirling low and then climbing into steep registers of sky, where it half-swoons like the high notes of a saxophone solo.

"Kirei," Hiroshi says quietly, his eyes also following the hypnotic flight of the albatross, which twitches its tail a few times.

"Why are they called short-tailed albatrosses?" I ask. "Their tails don't look unreasonably short." Without shifting their gaze, Hiroshi and Peter smile.

"It's because of the way their feet stick out," Peter explains. "A large bird needs long legs and big feet for takeoffs from water. In fact, sometimes, if the wind isn't quite right, they'll run for about fifty yards or so and give up. The tail appears smaller than it really is, but that's an illusion. They could just as well be called the long-legged albatross."

"It would perhaps be better to call them by their other name—Steller's albatross," Hiroshi says. "Especially since a number of the animals named by Steller—who was a great naturalist—have now become extinct." Pulling a notebook from his pocket, Hiroshi begins taking the year's census of birds, eggs, mated pairs. Peter takes out his sketchbook and soon fills two pages with courting pairs of albatrosses caught in the midst of telltale gestures. An albatross passes over our heads, and the wind rushing loudly through its feathers sounds exactly like the distant roar of a 747. At last it reefs in low over the high village, stretches its feet down even farther, as if somehow to telescope them to the ground, does a head-to-toe twitch arpeggio with umbrellaed wings, and lands in a series of recovered falls, which ends only when it somersaults into a back flop. We laugh. Albatrosses are great courtiers, great aerobats, but also great buffoons.

By midafternoon, the birds who spent the morning feeding at sea return to their colonies. One by one, they enter the fortress skies to form a giant "kettle" overhead—a bubbling of birds. As one dives down, finds a calm, drops anchor, and lands, another slips in on top of the thick stew of albatrosses now circling, angling, diving, wheeling, sliding across the sky. Wings spread, they make black crosses against the silver sea. An albatross sails in low over our heads, drops its feet, reefs in its wings, cuts close to the ground, only to be lifted again by an updraft. It spreads its wings and sails around for another try, misses again, sails around once more, braking with its feet, swooping and turning, in desperation heading in close to the cliff face to get a stall effect, which finally works. In twenty attempts at landing, it did not flap its wings even once.

The albatrosses seem so safe and at ease in this rocky cloister. Every one of them is descended from a few who were at sea when their brethren were killed. Once young birds are fledged, they go to sea and will remain there for from three to five years. Some young birds that had left the island, escaping both the bludgeoning by the feather hunters and the volcanic eruptions, were the progenitors of all the birds we see today. If, unlike other albatrosses, these birds are wary of humans, it's understandable. Fowlers started coming to Torishima in 1897 to harvest the feathers, and by 1900 there was a thriving settlement of 300 people. When the volcano erupted in 1902, there were 125 people in the village, and all of them died under a boiling mantle of lava. But other fowlers came to replace them, and continued arriving until the 1920s, when there were no longer enough albatrosses to make a permanent village worthwhile. In 1933, a Japanese edict declared Torishima off-limits. But in 1932 the fowlers, knowing that they were soon going to lose a favorite hunting ground, set out for one final slaughter. This massacre reduced the number of birds from a workable breeding stock of about two thousand to only thirty to fifty individuals. In 1939, the volcano erupted again for the second time in this century. The Moon Desert, which had once been a favorite nesting ground of the short-tailed albatross, was charred to blowing cinders. During World War II, the government built a garrison on the island, and the men reported sighting only one albatross. In 1949, Oliver Austin, an American ornithologist, circumnavigated the island in a Japanese whaler but did not see any albatrosses at all, and he believed the bird to be extinct. In fact, there must have been a few hidden nests, perhaps no more than four or five. A few birds were spotted in 1950. In the autumn of 1965 there were many earthquakes, and the personnel from the weather station were evacuated.

Alone at last in their stone citadel, the impoverished family of short-tailed albatrosses gradually began to rally. Conservationists made sure the species was internationally recognized as endangered by the International Council for Bird Preservation, which held a congress in Tokyo in 1960. This led the Japanese government to designate the short-tailed albatross a national monument in 1962. When Hiroshi became involved with the project, he threw himself into it like a dynamo. On November 17, 1976, he made his first trip to Torishima, and he has returned at least twice a year ever since, to study the birds, monitor their progress, and do what he can to help them recover. In 1956, there were just twelve reported nests. But in 1988, eighty-nine eggs were laid.

This may sound like a success story. But short-tailed albatrosses are still desperately endangered. If the volcano should erupt again, as it could at any time, and the area where we now sit should be destroyed, it is unlikely that the albatrosses would be able to nest anywhere else on the island. Breeding would stop. So it is crucial that the albatrosses be attracted to as many other sites as possible. Hiroshi hopes that if the birds can be persuaded to multiply well on Torishima, they will seek nesting colonies on other islands, too. On the leeward Hawaiian islands, short-tailed albatrosses have been spotted sitting alongside black-footed and Laysan albatrosses; and they have been seen on Minami-Kojima in the Senkaku Islands. But they haven't been seen nesting in either locale.

Although Hiroshi has been their knight errant and keen observer, the short-tailed albatrosses remain a feathered mystery. Because there are so few birds, it's difficult even to chart their seasonal movements. But we do have a few scraps of information about their habits, in particular, and much more is known about the habits of albatrosses in general. In early October, the short-tailed albatrosses return to Torishima and congregate offshore for a few days, and then start landing on this small platform at the base of the cliffs. Albatrosses live long lives—on the average, from forty to sixty years. Each bird one sees is a long-term inhabitant of the planet. They are monogamous, and a pair will rendezvous at the previous year's nest site. A young bird will return to the island after two or three years at sea and begin the baroque courtship display that ensures a tight pair bonding. Young birds may not understand how to copulate, but they often try it anyway, even if it means sitting on the head instead of the tail by mistake. What they're doing in their early years is practicing romance and learning how to set up a home. The courtship display—which they must perfect to such a razor-fine finesse that they can dance in unison as one rapture, one yearning—is necessary to bring the pair to a pitch of arousal where copulation can occur. Intercourse itself lasts only about thirty or forty seconds in albatrosses. The extravagant buildup is everything.

When the pairs go to sea, they don't stick together; and individuals may fly as far as the west coast of North America or the Bering Sea. The male returns two to four days ahead of the female, recognizes her on sight, and greets her with ceremonial bows. Then they indulge in courtship rituals for a few weeks, and she lays an egg in late October or early November. She lays only one egg per season—a large, dull white egg about six times the size of a chicken egg, which weighs around three quarters of a pound—and incubation lasts sixty-four or sixty-five days. The female usually sits on the egg for about three weeks, and then the male eagerly spells her and sits for about twenty-two days. During this time, the parent stands up and turns the egg every few hours. Of course, it can't leave the nest to eat or drink. During that long fast the albatross can lose around 20 percent of its weight. The female relieves the male for another twenty-two-day shift. As the day of hatching approaches, the two birds get very excited, almost pushing each other off the nest, as if each wants to be the one to finally hatch the egg. This is also a period of heavy billing, preening, and nuzzling.

After the egg hatches, one of the adults always stands guard to brood the chick and protect it from the ravages of the elements—sun, dust, storms, and so on—as well as from would-be predators. There aren't enough albatrosses left on Torishima to sustain a population of serious predators, but in the old days, jungle crows and ticks accounted for about a third of all chick deaths. These days the culprit is mainly inexperience. Birds sometimes accidentally knock an egg out of the nest, and once that egg is out, it might as well be a sock or a snowball—the bird has no idea what it is and won't retrieve it.

All albatrosses feed their young by regurgitation. The parents fly over the ocean at night and fish for shrimp and squid, which come to the surface and leave a wide, luminous trail behind them. Albatrosses do not feed on the wing, though. When one sees prey, it skids to a halt in the water, simply paddles like a barnyard duck, and with one deft movement of its long hooked bill, snatches up the morsel. Sky-roaming nomads, they feed farther from their chicks than any other birds. Indeed, some color-coded albatrosses have been recorded feeding 2,400 miles from their nesting site. They may take to the ocean to forage for up to fourteen days at a time, storing the partly digested food in a special hamper at the top of the stomach. When they return, they regurgitate food to their chicks. After two or three weeks both parents are needed to feed the chick, whose demands grow, but by that time the chick can safely be left alone while the adults go off to feed.

By May or June, the adult albatrosses gradually start to lose interest in parenthood, and they desert the plump young chick, which now looks like a rangy brown volcano. Sometimes a chick will sit around on the island for two weeks, losing weight and testing its wings, until at last, unaided, untutored, it sets off on its first flight. In Hiroshi's office we saw a film he made of a chick taking its first flight with much clumsy stumbling and trepidation. Facing into the wind, it sprinted with its big feet across the slopes of Torishima, wings out, running for forty yards or so, until suddenly its wobbly legs began to dance, its wings floated like a parasol on a windy street, and with a wild-eyed look of self-astonishment, it coasted out over the sea. How poignant it must be for Hiroshi to watch his avian family fly, year after year, knowing that he's not going to see the chicks again for at least two years, and possibly not for four or five years.

When the light starts to fail at day's end, we reluctantly pack up to leave. Soon the cliffs will be full of nesting shadows, and climbing back up to the land of humans will be too difficult. We must go, but we would prefer to stay, camped out at the edge of this natural stage, watching albatrosses coast among the Gothic spires of rock. Being close to albatrosses is an experience somewhere between the spiritual and the sexual. As their whinnying cries fill the air behind us, we hoist our burdens and start the long climb.

When we return to camp, we find the government team is back and busy with dinner, so we unpack and take seats around the low table. We laugh when we see the banquet being spread before us; expeditions usually mean canned goods and stale bread. Tonight there is pepper steak, rice, barbecued fish, freshly prepared sushi, and fresh vegetables. Then the cook brings round a platter of cooked limpets. A delicacy, they are dense and gristly, reminding me of the inside of a horse's hoof—including the stones. Mandarin oranges and beer and strong Japanese spirits follow. Overhead, five bird constellations watch us in silence—the Crane, the Swan, the Phoenix, the Peacock, the Eagle—from their stone-cold aviary among the stars. Peering into the well of night, my gaze tumbles toward deep space, and back in time, toward the first feathery tantrums of the universe. My craft is so small, I think, and the ocean is so wide. Exhausted, at last, from the long day's rigors, everyone wanders into the bunker, crawls into a sleeping bag, and waits with eyes closed for the generator out back to run down, so that the lightbulb inside the bunker will fade for the night.

No alarm sounds, but at precisely three minutes to six, all of the men wake up, stretch their arms wide, and then, one by one, drift lazily out of the bunker. The cook yawns, tucks in his shirt, puts a large kettle on the gas burner. We eat breakfast quickly, excited to be heading back to the fortress. Though Hiroshi's backpack looks even heavier today, he somehow manages to carry it cheerfully, taking the short, slow steps of a man on a long journey with a heavy load. Once more, we climb up past the abandoned weather-station barracks. The haunting notes of a plover drift across the morning as we hike over the lava lakes and through the fields of yellow chrysanthemums. Today the walk is faster and easier. The journey up is different from the journey down. While we're fresh, we climb steeply at first, then continue across the lava fields to the lap of Sulfur Peak, where the ground is hot to the touch and sulfur fumes dance in the lengthening light of dawn. Some areas of the earth look raw. Without the volcano, there would be no Tori-shima, and no refuge for the albatrosses. Throughout the oceans of the world, magma from the molten core of the earth pushes up to form volcanic islands like this one. The molten lava solidifies, becomes more stable, and slowly drifts, while other hot spots produce more volcanic islands, and soon there is a steaming archipelago. This is my first volcano, and I love watching the sulfur fumes dance like djinns.

As we climb across the pungent fields, I feel the warmth of the island's molten heart through my boots. Steam, like a dragon's breath, rises all around us. In the Moon Desert, where the lava sand blows, each footstep leaves a cloud, as if one's life force were burning right through the soles of one's feet. Yesterday we left pouches of water at this spot, and I fall to my knees and hold one of them overhead, pour a long gush of water down my throat, and wash the black dust deeper inside me. Then we continue on through the narrow col. Soon we are at the edge of the fortress and begin climbing down. More tentative than yesterday, I find the first rope easier today. At the second, searching out good footholds, I slide down a rock with one foot, carry the second foot around, slide down to another ledge. The next toehold waits below. Stretching, I give the rope a little slack, stretch farther, lower myself, feel toward the spot, then—*bang!*—the floor shoots away underneath me, and spinning around, I fall backward, my left hand gripping the rope as I smash against sharp rock. Pain butts deep into my back. Below me, Hiroshi has already climbed out of sight. Peter, vigilant nearby, looks calm but ready to spring.

"I'm hurt," I call, and the words come out as a long moaning.

He rushes to me, where, in mid-cliff, I am wedged in a colander of rocks, and he says, "Breathe deeply. That's better. Get some air in."

"I think I've cracked a rib." Looking down at the cliff below, then up at the cliff above, I wonder, How will I get out of here?

Perched below me, Peter checks the best route down. Although I know it's going to be painful, I must somehow turn around and hold on to the rope tightly with my left hand. My hands are what will save me. I turn and grasp the rope. That small movement sends lightning forks through my chest and back. Peter calls out footholds.

"Stretch your right foot down to where my feet are," he says. I do. "Now move your left foot below you to an open space beside those two narrow rocks." He steps down six inches. "Right foot just above where my right foot is . . ." And so we climb down to where the rock face quits and the lava hill begins. There, struggling to keep my torso straight, I put my hands on his backpack and follow him slowly down to the bottom of the dune.

Hiroshi runs forward, anxious and sympathetic. The two men try to pinpoint the pain bleating low on my left side, which has made it impossible to bend at the waist—or cough, speak loudly, sneeze, or laugh, as I soon discover. I will be doomed to a life of shallow breaths for some weeks. Guiding me up onto the crest of the lava dune which is our lookout point, they dig a pit, brace it with knapsacks, and settle me into the hole. Later I will learn that I have broken three ribs—complete breaks, with the rib spars lying parallel to one another. For months, I will not be able to lie down or stand up by myself, and pain will be my constant companion. But when I watch the albatrosses coast overhead, holding the sky upon their wings, filled with the restless ongoing of their flight, I would not trade my lot for anyone's. Life is too full of easy entrances and exits. The birds need their fortress, which is all that has saved them. I do not welcome this pain, gnawing like a wolf pack, but if that is the toll that must be paid, then it is well spent. Taking a breath, I laugh quietly to myself. No wonder they have survived here. I am proof that their fortress works.

At twilight, when like monks we finish our silent beholding, which for me is a form of prayer, we gather up our knapsacks and consider the ascent. Hampered by a tight straitjacket of pain, I cannot move the left side of my body; yet somehow we must climb back up the cliffs. Hiroshi loops a guide rope high around my shoulders, and Peter lifts me bodily. We are a good team, in calm and in distress. Working together, the three of us finally emerge from the fortress and climb wearily back down toward camp.

"A great day, despite everything," I tell them, and I mean it. "Who would drink from a cup when they can drink from the source?"

The next morning, Peter and Hiroshi set off by themselves, the government men prepare to leave on a chartered boat, and I spend the day in camp. The pain has gotten much worse, and I can feel bones shifting like mah-jongg tiles when I inhale. Soon a fever begins, and will not relent under an assault of aspirin, acetaminophen, and antibiotics. The closest hospital is eighteen hours away by fishing boat. I know breaking your ribs can swiftly lead to pneumonia, and as my fever soars, I drift in and out of consciousness. In lucid moments, I consider grim possibilities. I may die on this remote island, alone in a stone bunker, far from home and loved ones. When one of the engineers returns for his gear, I whisper the Japanese for "Help." Using pantomime and a few words from a Japanese phrase book, I tell him, "Sick. Broken inside. Please, find Hiroshi and Peter. With albatrosses. Please go fast, fast." I give him a short note to deliver. When the runner leaves, I wrap myself in a heap of clothing and blankets and wait. A young Japanese woman arrives—I do not know if she is real or a hallucination. She feels my burning head, takes off her white shirt and washes my face with it, fills the shirt with ice—Where did the ice come from?—and lays it across my forehead. Then she disappears. Deep within the bunker, I watch a few rays of sunlight construe the narrow room. The outside world trembles with light. I dream of blinding-white albatrosses, whose yellow heads sparkle as they whirl in the twilight like an unnamed constellation. Suddenly a shape appears at the door. Panting, sweat pouring off him, his hair slicked back like a steel helmet, Peter looks as if he had just fallen down a birth canal. Taking off his pack, he sits down, and we discuss the various ways off the island. The safest is to go on the government charter boat, which will be leaving soon. The fever is steep and mysterious, and we must act quickly. He has already said good-bye to Hiroshi, who stayed behind at the fortress, at his post with the albatrosses, where he belongs.

An hour later, we climb aboard a boat three times as large as the one that ferried us to Torishima. This one, only two months old, gleams with stainless-steel fittings, pile carpets, and sleeping bunks. A charter boat, it cruises the islands to the north, mainly on scuba-diving and fishing trips. The mystery woman who bathed me with her shirt is a crewmember, and the captain has radioed ahead for an ambulance to meet us at dockside. Before heading north, the captain circumnavigates the island, which gives us a fine view of the bolts of lava where the village was washed into the sea.

Sulfur Peak stretches up raggedly, as if to pipette the blue sky. At last, the fortress of the *ahodori* drifts into view, with its cantilevered walls, amphitheater of jagged rock, and small green apron dotted with white. Surrounded by the frozen cascades of rock, the birds look delicate and fragile.

"The world's entire population of nesting short-tailed albatrosses," Peter says sadly. A moment later, he grins broadly. We both do, feeling the same indelible thrill at having seen them. "Look, there's Hiroshi!" He points to a lone figure sitting on a dune of lava underneath a snowstorm of soaring birds. We wave to him, and Hiroshi lifts his hat and waves back. As the boat turns north, and the sun begins to set in a thick welter of clouds, a recording of "Auld Lang Syne" gushes from the loudspeaker. Short-tailed albatrosses swoop and slide across the wave crests. One dives just off the bow of the boat, picking up speed as it enters the realm of calm air. Now it turns across the wind, skates behind a wave, and then tips its wing, turns up, and rises fast, almost vertically, behind the wave crest, tilts around, and then starts across the wind once again, zigzagging at colossal speed. For some time, we stand in the glow of the setting sun and watch the albatross cartwheel over the waves, changing from white when it's framed by the dark water to black when it's framed by the paler sky. Positive and negative, it dives from the transparent air down to the thick gelid water and up again, lacing the sea and sky together with its swooping flight. It is the wind's way of thinking about itself. At last, it flies straight down the sun street and out toward the horizon, under a tumultuous bruise of sky, where shadow haikus dance on the water, and disappears into a bright kingdom of clouds.

GOLDEN LION
TAMARINS

❖

*In summer, at the National Zoo in
Washington, D.C., golden lion tamarins run
free in the park, climbing on rope pathways
through the treetops. In time, they will be flown
to Brazil and turned loose in the rain forest, and
the zoo hopes that while they are in Washington,
they will develop the skills necessary to survive in
the wild. But animals raised in zoos lack many of
their natural behaviors. For example, these
golden lion tamarins have to be taught how to
deal with disappointment, how to fulfill their
nature and discover themselves as primates. They
must be taught to thrive as monkeys, because
when all the daily trials of life in the forest are
missing, the instincts forged by those trials
disappear too. What does this tell us about the
necessity for stress, ambiguity, struggle? A
captive life is also a stress-free life, but the longer
one lives in a reduced state, the more reduced
one becomes. There are no predators, but there is
also no sense of escape or salvation, no hunger,
but also no thrill of accomplishment. Golden
lion tamarins are monogamous, with strong
rivalries and soap-opera-like sex dramas. Some
of their family problems seem only too human,
offering a hint of what life may have been like
for our early ancestors. Because I find such
mysteries irresistible, and because golden lion*

*tamarins are among the most beautiful and most
endangered creatures on earth, I decided to lend
a hand with the reintroduction project, and
accompany tamarin families to Brazil, in the
hope that they would be fruitful and multiply.*

⋘◇⋙

In the rain forest, no niche lies unused. No emptiness goes unfilled. No gasp of sunlight goes untrapped. In a million vest pockets, a million life-forms quietly tick. No other place on earth feels so lush. Sometimes we picture it as an echo of the original Garden of Eden—a realm ancient, serene, and fertile, where pythons slither and jaguars lope. But it is mainly a world of cunning and savage trees. Truant plants will not survive. The meek inherit nothing. Light is a thick yellow vitamin they would kill for, and they do. One of the first truths one learns in the rain forest is that there is nothing fainthearted or wimpy about plants. They are aggressive about self-defense. Some trees protect their circulatory systems by putting a layer of strychnine or quinine under their bark. Others have poisonous sap, leaves, or berries. There are tannins and scents that mimic insect juvenile hormones and enzymes strong enough to tenderize meat (or your tongue), and agents powerful enough to paralyze a wayward insect or animal. One ingenious plant is the *Derris* vine, whose bark Amazonian Indians crush in the river to poison fish. Some plants develop colorful red-speckled or streaked leaves so that they appear to be dying or dead and therefore of no interest to hungry mouths. Others evolve long vicious spines. *Strychnos* can stop your heart with its beauty . . . or its curare. And then, of course, there are the hallucinogens, produced by tree and vine bark, flowers, beans, cacti, and fungi. Some of the toads are hallucinogenic, too, which isn't at all surprising when you look at their burst of free-floating hop-and-color squatting on a branch, brazenly daring you to touch. On a rain-forest walk, I found a vibrant aqua-blue-and-yellow arrowhead frog that was covered with a poisonous mucus. Tiny but pungent with death, it sat right out on a felled tree and let me get close enough to breathe on it.

In temperate northern forests, one finds fewer species of plants in an area, but many of each species; it's not unusual to see large glades of hemlock or maple. But in the rain forest, there are kaleidoscopic numbers of different species, and very few samples of each one. When you look at such a forest, it has depth, texture, variety. Yet the members of each species are spaced far apart. There is not much breeze to carry seeds about. It's hard to have a sex life when you can't move, so jungle plants have become incredible tricksters and manipulators, conning others into performing sex acts with them. In a rain forest, it's no use spilling their seed on the ground beneath them. There would be too much inbreeding, and one of the best aspects of sex, from a plant's point of view, is that it freshens the gene pool. So plants lure hummingbirds, bees, bats, butterflies, moths, insects. Plants are willing to dress up in animal disguises. Some plants are carnivores. They are not mild-mannered, even if they aren't quick-footed. They are promiscuous, and they will stoop to every low-down trick. They would dress up in a gorilla suit if they could.

Some orchids, for example, living high up in the canopies, have learned how to divert bees with their splashy color and blossoms that lure the unsuspecting bee to brush up against their sex organs. Other orchids have evolved to mimic the female tachinid fly, so that males will try to mate with them and end up dusted with pollen. Still other orchids mimic the territorial movements of a male *Centris* bee and need only wait for passing males to take up the fight. Sex or violence will do equally well: whether the orchids are courted or fought with, they rub pollen on the visitor. Some of the best pollinators are male orchid bees, which are bright metallic blue or green and are after not pollen but fragrances, which they use as part of an aphrodisiac brew and store in pockets on their hind legs. Going from flower to flower, they collect a note of fragrance and blend it in their hind-leg pockets; at some magical point, the mix begins to simmer just right, and they become such Adonises that even other males take notice. Soon, a swarm of brightly flashing males dancing in the sunlight attracts female orchid bees, just as the flowers attracted the males. Now the males are the beautiful, fragrant blossoms of the jungle. Who could resist them?

No other place on earth is as biologically complex as the rain forest. Animals swerve and flutter through dense walls of green. The riot of lushness comes in part from hanging mosses, ferns, cacti, orchids, vines, and bromeliads. Each tree is a palimpsest of other plants. Most plants one sees hanging on to trees are not parasites; they merely use the trees as a perch. Ninety percent of the world's vines live in the rain forest, and the lianas can grow as large as a human leg and lie like glutted snakes on the floor. Each sunrise, the bird chorus sounds like a rehearsal of a Charles Ives symphony. Howler monkeys yodel as they swing among the trees. One can find three-toed sloths, jaguars, bats, bamboo rats, owls, rhinoceros beetles, hummingbirds, coral snakes, large lizards and rodents, wild dogs, giant spiders, African bees, and legions of lesser-known, rarely observed insects and birds.

This extraordinary habitat is also the home of the golden lion tamarin, the most beautiful monkey in the world, a sunset-and-cornsilk-colored creature that lives nowhere else on earth. Not long ago, I paid a visit to Russell Mittermeier, director of Conservation International and a lifelong explorer of rain forests. He raved about golden lion tamarins. "Their color is magnificent," he said. "They're really spectacular-looking mammals. When the Jesuit chronicler of Magellan's voyage around the world first saw these monkeys in the sixteenth century, he described them as 'simian-like cats similar to small lions,' and that's how they got their name. Although they're tiny animals, they have a striking aspect to them: they really do look like mini-lions. And baby golden lion tamarins are the most appealing creatures you can imagine. They have this innocent look on their faces—a *Where am I?* sort of look. Let me tell you, when a tiny golden thing about the size of your fist sits there looking so lost, it brings out your parenting instincts fast." Large nuclear families of these monkeys once roamed through the canopies, eating fruits and insects, sleeping in night nests, raising their young. Now only about four hundred survive in the wild. "That's really scary," Mittermeier said. "You can find that many cats or dogs in a city block in Manhattan. But that's the world's population of this unique animal." A global effort is under way to save them, in part because they are what's called a flagship species. Like the panda or koala, golden lion tamarins live in an endangered ecosystem. Not only they but their entire world may go extinct.

The Mata Atlantica is a narrow strip of rain forest that stretches for a thousand miles along the northeast coast of Brazil; because it is separated from the Amazon by a mountain range, its plants and animals are unique. But, as in the Amazon region, its trees have fallen to bulldozers and farmers. Only islands of vegetation remain, broken up by roads, dams, towns, and large farms (fazendas). From historic accounts of the area, we know that only 2 percent of the original forest remains. The hard truth is that it hasn't disappeared because of malice or catastrophe—people simply wished to improve their lives. In North America, we destroyed our own frontiers and wildernesses in a similar way. Progress is a hungry giant. What many people don't realize is that in the rain forest, most of the nutrients are in the trees, not the soil, and there are no extras, no backups. As soon as something dies, it returns immediately into the living system by rotting. It doesn't linger in the soil, or become the soil, as in temperate regions. Either the rains wash it away, or mycorrhizal fungi convert it at once and it returns to the trees. The living tumult of insects helps, too. But there is no use trying to farm the land, or graze cattle on it. Because the richness lives only in the trees, if the trees vanish, the whole ecosystem will collapse.

I hear them before I see them: short warbling birdsong followed by a whole note played on a flute, then spasmodic chuckings, a sudden trill, another long call. Parrots? Thrushes? What is a flock of birds doing at the Rio de Janeiro airport's cargo terminal? As five tan "Veri-kennel Convertible Pet Apartments" are unloaded at my feet, each one perforated with small breathing holes, I realize that the holes have turned the boxes into wind instruments. A jungle of tuneful clamor pours from them. Squatting, I peek into the straw-clotted shadows of one box at vague flashes of color and jostling fur. Again the birdsong, louder this time and more urgent. Inside, a family of golden lion tamarins, sent from the National Zoo in Washington, D.C., huddles together and calls to their neighbors in the other boxes. Even their murmurs chime.

"They're safe and sound," Ben Beck says with relief. A solid man in his fifties, with salt-and-pepper hair, a meticulously trimmed beard, and a quiet take-charge way about him, Ben heads the Golden Lion Tamarin Reintroduction Project. Now that so few of these monkeys remain, the National Zoo breeds them in captivity and walks them by hand back out into the forest. Twice a year, Beck flies to Brazil with complete GLT families, or with a spouse for a Brazilian GLT that's come of age. Our group on this trip also includes his wife, Beate, a petite, tawny-haired woman with a light German accent, who has worked with monkeys for many years; Joleen, a thirty-one-year-old primate keeper from the Brookfield Zoo in Chicago (which has sent one of the family groups); Howard, a tall, bearded photographer from Brookfield Zoo; and Alfie, a primatologist based at the National Zoo who specializes in fossils and teeth. We are met by some of the Brazilians who live and work at the field station: Fernando, who manages the project locally; Andrea, who directs its daily work, feeding the monkeys, sending out the teams of observers; and Denise, a combination of educator and diplomat, who teaches schoolchildren about tamarins, acts as a liaison with local farmers, and helps the government find and repatriate stolen monkeys. So beautiful are the tamarins, which sell illegally for as much as twenty thousand dollars, that hunters will often risk a two-year prison sentence to steal one. One key to the Tamarin project is how well it fits into the daily life of its neighbors. Twenty-two of the project's employees come from nearby towns, which makes the program important for the local economy. Near the main highway, an education building with attached museum shows films and offers books and pamphlets, posters and T-shirts. Locals may fear the deep forest, but they take pride in living beside a natural wonder. Of course, a golden monkey, beautiful and fascinating in its own right, helps to personalize the plight of the rain forest. For many people, there is something too out-of-control, too gushing, about nature, something that frightens by sheer excess. Their second fear (dying is their first) is that they might somehow become as plural as all they survey. When they imagine the dense green lungs of the jungle, they feel suffocated and panicky. They need a gentle familiar, a spirit guide, a focus for their concern. In this rain forest, one finds many endangered birds, insects, frogs, snakes, and plants, but they're not as cute and cuddly as a shimmering golden monkey—

especially one that is monogamous, family-loving, and easy to identify with. The golden lion tamarin wears a human face.

"This is the most dangerous part of our job," Ben says, grinning, as we drive north along the two-lane highway that has opened the Mata Atlantica up to civilization. Cars and trucks typically speed four abreast, use the road shoulders as passing lanes, and often lose their axles in yard-deep potholes. Young boys stand along the roadway, selling wads of dried, pressed bananas. We pass dozens of ceramics plants. Terra-cotta roof tiles are a big industry in this part of Brazil; the factories are fueled by rain forest trees.

In time, the strip of fast-food joints, barbecue restaurants, and businesses gives way to rangy farmlands and forested knolls. Ahead we see a mountain range—the edge of the Atlantic coastal forest, the fragile margin of a continent. It is against Brazilian law to cut down rain forest at the top of a mountain because the trees prevent terrible erosion and mud slides. The mountaintop forests remain to protect the farmers, but, inadvertently, they have saved the forest creatures in small floating islands of vegetation. At a sign marked RESERVA BIOLÓGICA POÇO DAS ANTAS, we turn onto a dirt road and follow it for twenty minutes through farmland, swamp, and then forest, to a palm-lined drive and a large white stucco house.

Once a goat barn, the house was rebuilt by the first researchers. Now it looks large and inviting, with a swelling purple bougainvillea at the front steps, a herb garden, a barbecue pit, and breadfruit, lime, and banana trees. Inside, a small kitchen opens onto a dining room dominated by a long table, whose top is an irregular slab of local wood polished to a high gloss. Two small bedrooms, each with four bunk beds, serve as men's and women's dorms. A toilet and shower stall are across the hall. Most people gather on the open-sided back porch, where four black car seats have been arranged as couches. Clotheslines hang above them. Against the wall, a blackboard gives the week's schedule, and beside that a worktable holds tools, monkey feeders, and miscellaneous fixings. A pegboard stores raincoats, with wet mud-clotted boots arranged neatly below. Smells of mildew, ripe bananas, dog-food-like "Monkey Diet," free-roaming chickens, car exhaust, and wildflowers mix in the air.

Work starts right away. Our monkeys need temporary lodgings. A family of wild golden lion tamarins would normally sleep huddled together in a tree hole or a thick nest of vines. Three large cages nestled in the forest at our front door will be their halfway houses. We begin by filling the cages with branches, bromeliads, and lengths of bamboo. Then we hang a water bowl from one branch and small partially peeled bananas from another. A few shoebox-shaped wire traps also hold bananas. If the monkeys can be habituated to the traps, they'll be easier to catch once they're in the wild. Then we fit each cage with a "nest box," a large blue-and-white Igloo ice chest that has been specially adapted for the monkeys. Tamarins prefer duplex homes, to give them a little variety and to protect them against predators. So the nest boxes have been divided into two rooms, an upper and a lower, with an almond-shaped door leading into the top story. A tamarin that wants privacy can generally find it, and if an ocelot reaches into the top of the nest, the tamarins can dash to the bottom.

As we arrange all the bits and pieces of the tamarins' new world, the cage starts to look like one of Joseph Cornell's collage boxes, or a Christmas tree minus the tree. Andrea wires the last ornament into place—a large, square feeder whose technical name is "portable micromanipulator platform." The locals just call it a *comidoro*. Like an oversized scaffolding of Tinkertoys, its five plastic pipes are riddled with evenly spaced holes and filled with a variety of chopped-up fruits and chunks of the Monkey Diet. The *comidoro* makes it possible to feed the monkeys, but it also trains them to insinuate their long slender fingers into tight places to search for food.

Across the compound, the monkeys quietly call to one another, and we hear their uncertain voices echoing through the yard. They're lucky to be here. At the last minute, they were nearly left behind. This summer Chicago's Brookfield Zoo (which has been successfully breeding tamarins for many years) sent the National Zoo a family of monkeys to return to the wild. But, when they arrived, a vet discovered that Flash, the breeding male, had a positive blood titer for a hepatitis-like virus. This wasn't unusual—human adults often carry positive antibodies to mumps or measles, which they were exposed to as youngsters, without being able to infect anyone. So they assumed Flash was safe, but they quarantined him anyway. None of the other monkeys showed any signs of the illness. A week ago, the zoo's pathologist positively identified the virus as one that causes hemorrhagic fever, a rodent-borne illness that can also afflict people. Rumor had it that the infected animals could be Typhoid Marys—although not appearing to be ill themselves, they might pass the virus on to others. Suppose the male died and was scavenged by rodents, which in turn were eaten by other rodents, porcupines, or oceleots, and an epidemic started that threatened the whole rain forest? How could the zoo expose the last golden lion tamarins to a plague? Three days ago, Ben decided not to risk bringing Flash. The rest of the group came—but now they need a breeding male.

"This was a total ringer for me," Ben says as he adjusts the wiring on the *comidoro*. "What to do? Well, I found a young male already in Brazil who was just coming to breeding age. He's not ideal—we like males to have had experience in child rearing before they start their own families. But we checked his genes, to make sure there wouldn't be too much inbreeding, and he's a good mate for this Brookfield female."

At the National Zoo, a "golden lion tamarin studbook" functions as an old-fashioned family Bible, chronicling all the marriages and offspring of GLTs throughout the world. A computer check gives keepers "the coefficient of inbreeding"—a key to lineage and genetic diversity. Circumstances don't always allow genetic mixing to take place. This is especially the case among zoo populations, where the animals can become too closely related and lose the variety needed for a strong immune system. Some wild animals—the cheetah is perhaps the best-known and saddest case—are so inbred that extinction is almost certain. Because the world's cheetahs have identical DNA, they're essentially clones of one another. To thrive, a species must be larger than any one individual, but with cheetahs each individual is the whole species. Any virus that can kill one of them can kill all of them. Because wild golden lion tamarins are developing a similar problem, zoos mate them carefully and even use birth control in some groups to ensure a strong bloodline.

When the Brazilian male joins the Brookfield female and children, he'll be a "veteran greenhorn," a reintroduced monkey who already knows the ropes, and that will help the newcomers adapt. Already savvy to the rain forest, he'll search out insects from twisted palm leaves, orient himself well among the branches, and be alert to predators. Although he won't consciously teach them skills, they'll learn faster by watching him.

"Okay. Let's go get the monkeys," Ben says at last, and we fetch one of the pet kennels, carry it into the cage, and open its door. A streak of yellow, the mother leaps out uncertainly, runs to the familiar smell of the nest box, and dives in. Her four offspring follow, making high smooching sounds as they poke their heads out and eye their new surroundings. The babies look like little troll dolls with wild manes, radiant skin, rubbery faces, and round eyes black as Sen-Sen. Mother looks more like a Kabuki dancer, with slightly Oriental eyes, crepey skin, and a strong chin. As the kids creep out to explore the cage, they make steady "contact calls" that mean something like "Hey, I'm here! Where are you?" "I'm here, too. Who else is here?" One of the kids finds a banana and utters a high-pitched trill. Soon all of them are eating. The locale looks strange, but at least the family is together and there's food and even the reassuring scent of their beds. Their lower jaws drop open to reveal sharp teeth as they bleat their long calls. Then they drag their rumps along the branches, scent-marking from chest and anal glands. A rich aroma of musk sweetens the air. Soon the cage will be completely decorated with smell—their only possession—and the new will become more familiar. Andrea whistles and chucks, and a kid chucks quietly back to her.

Returning to the porch for a second kennel, we carry Marty, a two-year-old male from the Brookfield Zoo, and give him a cage all by himself near a lime tree. In the forest, a grave tragedy happened last year. A tamarin family from Los Angeles was getting on splendidly in their new world when poachers stole the mother and father to sell as pets. This left four orphans: a young female, a young male, and a pair of twins only two months old. The older brother and sister have been raising the twins as best they can, but they mustn't mate. So we'll remove the brother, give Marty to the sister as a mate, and hope that he'll adopt the younger kids and have more of his own.

Finally, we fetch the last tamarins and release them into a third cage. This group includes a still-fertile middle-aged mother, a teenage daughter, and a younger son and daughter. They need a father. Our plan is to capture a compatible forest male for them. Such matchmaking doesn't always work. Sometimes a betrothed pair take a real dislike to each other. But that happens rarely. A larger and philosophically more disturbing hurdle is that the animals raised in captivity have forgotten how to be monkeys.

When zoo-born tamarins are set free in the forest they become disoriented and helpless. They lose their way in dense thickets among the thorns and the lianas. Not knowing how to feed themselves or return to their families, many starve. Would we know how to survive on the African savanna? Zoo animals have not learned how to forage, elude predators, be spatial, decipher their surroundings. Place a banana in front of them and they won't know how to open it. Imagine having to teach a monkey how to open a banana! Most of all, they are not used to disappointment. In zoos, food arrives on schedule in easy-to-eat-from bowls or plates. In the rain forest, they must discover food—insects hiding in rolled palm leaves or under bark; fruits; small amphibians. Food moves sometimes, and comes in all sorts of shapes, and it may not be where they last found it. How do you teach a monkey not to be discouraged? They must also learn that some frogs and snakes are poisonous. Poisonous animals didn't share their cage in the zoo. And they must learn about falling. In zoos, they ran along sturdy branches, bars, or ropes; they clung to cage wires. Never were they more than a few feet from the ground. In the rain forest, twigs may snap, slime-coated vines may send them skidding, not all branches will hold their weight, and tree canopies arch hundreds of feet above the ground. In zoos, ground means benign keepers and a safe stable world where tamarins feel secure. Yet in the wild, it's the sky that will save them—the ground teems with jungle cats, human hunters, and other predators.

Wild tamarins lead lives of elaborate social rituals and tribal relationships. Acrobatic and analytical, they can take the measure of a forest and map the best feeding spots. Although they sometimes fight with neighboring groups, the battles hide a secret agenda. While the adults posture and rave, the juveniles play together and check out potential mates. They really haven't other socially sanctioned ways of meeting. It is the habit of golden lion tamarins to be monogamous and live in tight family groups, where the father helps to raise the offspring. When a daughter reaches puberty at about two years old, the mother drives her away to find her own family, so that incest won't occur; the father does the same with a mature son. Females almost always give birth to fraternal twins, and siblings help raise one another. Large families are the rule. Touch dominates their lives; when they're not feeding, they're playing together or grooming one another. Separated from their family, they can die of loneliness. Ben and his colleagues have spent many years studying them. Few of the reintroduced tamarins survive—70 percent die in the first year after release. That 30 percent live is the great success story of the project.

After we unpack and the monkeys have had time to settle into their new surroundings, we catch three tamarins in traps and carry them to the laboratory to receive radio collars. In her small cage, Jenny watches us quietly. I slide a wooden divider through the cage bars and press her against one end of the cage so that Andrea can give her an injection. Three minutes later, she tumbles asleep. Sliding my thumb and forefinger around the back of her neck, I tow her out of the cage. How soft and frail her throat feels. It is unnerving to hold the windpipe of a living thing tight enough to restrain it, but loose enough not to choke it. What delicate, just-this-side-of-deadly balance will do? As my fingers make their own decisions, I'm reminded of how many of life's processes require complex acts of inarticulate finesse. One rarely pauses to divine how to climb a ladder, swim, cross a busy street; muscles and joints make their own small trials and revisions. Jenny is not as cognitive as I am, but her body follows its own wisdom in the same way mine does. There was a time, not far away in the shadowy past of our species, when we looked, and even thought, a lot like her. How eerie it is to cradle a previous version of yourself in your arms.

Carrying Jenny across the room, I first set her on a scale—she weighs 630 grams—then lay her down on the worktable. Golden tufts of fur stick out between her fingers and toes, which have small round pads at the base of each claw. Her long, slender fingers were made for reaching into narrow places, where insects may lurk. I have seen lithe, graceful hands like these in paintings of Thai dancers. Stroking the dark footpads, I'm surprised to discover them soft and yielding. Sensitivity is costly. Her vulnerable soles will open a world of details to her, but at what price? Thorns, stinging ants, bees, sharp bamboo, all could be dangerous. Unlike many monkeys, GLTs don't have prehensile tails; the long tail serves as a balance bar. On her small nose, two thin nostrils angle away from each other. A slight upside-down curve is the natural shape of her mouth, as if she were caught in a perpetual pout. Gold whiskers sprout from her chin, and a widow's peak of canary yellow leads to a full golden mane encircling the head. Her tiny guitar-pick-shaped tongue, flicking in and out, has a deep groove down the center, where most of the taste buds lie. Golden lion tamarins give off such a pungent odor that it's one of the ways to identify them, by depth of smell. Burying my nose in her chest, I inhale deeply the aroma of hot gingerbread mixed with drenched wheat. We jot down that her powerful smell is "average." Andrea fits her with the radio collar, a bow tie of electronics and antenna. Then I carry her to the sink and paint her tail with black dye. Picturing the tail in four sections, we mark monkeys according to a code, which makes it easier to identify them. Because she's the senior female, her whole tail will be black. Now Alfie begins his dentistry experiment, applying green latex to her teeth and taking an impression. What sharp canines. When I see a palate covered with ridges, I smile, because I have seen that pattern before, on dental casts of my own mouth. All primates have grooved palates. Finished with her at last, we set her back in a small cage so we can keep an eye on her until she wakes.

Then we "process" her daughter, Maria, in just the same way. But we're distressed to find a cut, like a small red badge, on her left shoulder. This pair, from the Columbia Zoo, has been quarreling worse than we thought.

"As long as there's no cut on the face, it's okay," Joleen says cautiously. "If there are cuts on the face, the fight's gotten serious enough for someone to get killed, because it means that one of the animals has become passive and isn't running away from attack."

At the moment, mother and daughter can't get out of each other's way, and we're hoping that tomorrow, when a male arrives for mother, daughter will become more pacific, and the whole family will settle down. Then we'll turn them loose in a fruit-laden forest. If their social bonds are sturdy and they adjust well to their new home, they should start breeding right away. In the wild, GLTs generally get pregnant once a year. But in especially rainy years, when fruit is plentiful, they sometimes get pregnant twice. Each time they give birth to fraternal twins, and it's those offspring who really master the rain forest. Reintroduced monkeys are typical immigrants, plagued by the usual array of immigrant problems. They don't adapt perfectly because there's too much that's new—sounds, foods, housing, predators, climate, disease, traffic patterns, educational needs. Their old-country dialect of habit and action doesn't quite work in this teeming new world. But their offspring will fit into this magical realm as perfectly as an incantation. The first generation born in a country belongs to it.

At five forty-five the following morning, the rooster begins loudly crowing, although gagging would be a more accurate description of the noise, since he sounds as if he's choking on lengths of flannel. The room is black as a mine shaft. After the fortieth crow, I stop counting and swing my foot out of bed, halting just in time as I recall that I'm in the top part of a bunk bed. Making my way to the kitchen, I light a candle and begin the ritual of coffee—boil water, toss grounds into it, bring it fast to another boil, drag it off the flame just as it's starting to boil over, and then drip it through a socklike cloth filter hanging from a tripod. Finally, I pour the coffee into two tall thermos bottles and help myself to a cupful. Strong, greasy, glycerin-black, Brazilian coffee packs a wallop, which sends me out to the porch as daylight is breaking. There I find Andrea and Beate, already preparing food for the monkeys.

"Bom dia!" Beate says. "Todo bem?" Good morning? Doing okay?

"Todo bem," I answer. Doing okay.

Because we're all worried about Jenny and Maria, we head down to their cage below the banana tree. Both of the females are out of the box, but Maria's fur is all puffed up, and her back is stiffly arched in a catlike show of aggression that's called an arch walk. Mother sits on a lower branch. Beate shakes her head. This is not good. In the wild, the mother would be dominating the daughter, but here, with no male on hand, the roles have somehow reversed. We wonder what will happen when a male is introduced. Only the breeding female of a family is fertile. Though middle-aged, the mother is still vital, and she would normally drive the daughter out to find her own family. Will she now stop being fertile and live out her days with the group as a dowager while the daughter takes reproductive control? Will they fight savagely enough to kill each other?

Back at the house, workers have begun arriving. One of them has found a hummingbird stunned on his car hood, and Ben holds its tiny, iridescent-green body, angling its long beak down to a dish of orange juice, which it laps with an even longer tongue. Soon it flies off by itself, and we climb into the van and go to meet the seven young men and women of the reintroduction team. At a crossroads near the main highway, wearing tan uniforms, they wait for us. Because we're a little late, they've used their machetes to carve a bench out of bamboo and vines, and there we find them "kicking stones," as Ben calls the art of waiting. They smile widely as we approach, and greet Ben and Beate with hugs and hand-shakes. All of them are in their twenties, fit and athletic, and this is a a full-time, six-days-a-week job for them. They share news about the monkeys, problems with poachers or fazenda owners, and concerns about their salary. Galloping inflation has gutted the Brazilian economy, their pay is in U.S. dollars, and the dollar keeps soaring and diving on their market. Ben assures them that wages will stay safely tied to the inflation rate. In a sense, their village, Silva Jardim, is a company town. The project hires twenty-two of its young people and also purchases a considerable amount of food and other supplies from the village, so it has fueled the local economy. Well paid and skilled, working for a noble cause, the members of the reintroduction team have prestigious jobs, and the town has adopted the project's Portuguese-speaking gringos.

When we leave, the team sets off for its day's work patrolling the many sites, and we drive to a neighboring fazenda, in whose forest a tamarin family from Seattle is living. We're hoping to trap the mature son, Seattle Six, who has grown too old to continue living at home. Mother has died. Father takes care of the kids, but the son needs to move out and start his own family, and the father needs a new bride. Low clouds hang like smoke in the valleys, and cecropia trees shimmer whitely from the hilltops as we drive down the rutted roads of a dairy farm. When the road runs out at the owner's palatial house, we leave our truck and begin climbing a steep hill up to the forest.

"This is the least progressive group," Ben says sadly as we finally leave the grassy hill behind and find ourselves facing a thick rain forest. Suddenly the air feels cool and wet. "They're not wild yet. We still give them food every third day."

Climbing through the undergrowth and along a stream, we at last find ourselves in monkey heaven—a sunstruck glade of tall trees and sweeping vines. Branches sway overhead, cicadas buzz, mosquitoes whine like dropping bombs, and gemlike humming-birds swoop among bird-of-paradise flowers. A tree frog clicks slowly, as if someone were winding up a toy. Yet there is an odd sense in which this jungle is almost a desert: there aren't grasses or herbs in the understory for animals to feed on. In fact, walking through the jungle one rarely sees any animals at all. Some are nocturnal. Many are camouflaged so well that one can pass by them as they lie in plain sight. But most animals mass overhead in the canopies, feeding on the foliage and banking the most valuable commodity of all, an element dangerously rare in such a dense forest, but one without which life can't survive—sunlight.

Everywhere you look in the jungle there are plants and animals desperate for a place in the sun, a piece of light: light, which is the golden rule of our planet; light, which raises the smallest leaf into a spiraling dance; light, which takes a black grotto or lay-by and dazzles it into a mossy green celebration. Light is the seductress of the forest, and one rarely finds gaudy flowers or many animals at lower levels. Instead, the enormous, dense canopies overhead contain the richest array of plant and animal life. Up high, the rain forest is a lush green jazz of flirting and mating, dueling and dancing, backstabbing and chicanery, con men and gold diggers, vamps and dandies. In the steamy tropical canopies, open blossoms drip with nectar, and epauletted bats puff up tufts of white fur on their shoulders as if they were inflating military insignia, to persuade females that they have more to give, that they are better endowed than the next bat, that they are larger than life. Birds do war dances and stripteases in reverse. The delirium of the jungle, drunk on sunlight and sex, is perpetually ashake with courting, mating, dueling, birthing, and mating again. Death happens often, but disappears quickly under the rain and hungry teeth, whereas the bluffing and strutting, cowering and crouching, bobbing and wooing, gathering and building, moaning and advertising continue day and night. Above us, an all-but-invisible pandemonium is under way. And yet what startles us is a sound completely out of place—undeniably the distant mooing of a cow.

"This is real-world conservation," Ben says, laughing, "beside a highway, on a hill past someone's cattle pasture. There's this romantic image people have of working in pristine environments. If the monkeys lived in a pristine environment, they wouldn't be in this mess."

He and Nelson set up a few traps for the monkeys, baiting them with bananas. Although we're hiding in the foliage, the monkeys have almost certainly been aware of us from the moment we entered the forest. Lichen-covered trees are spotted green, brown, and black, just as we are. Our camouflage pants blend with the greenery and dappled light. It's what we've adopted to look like trees, and it works. Small butterflies flit among the ferns, and then a giant blue one, with wings as large as two playing cards, kites by at eye level, stealing a gasp from all of us, and vanishes. In temperate forests, trees have leaves of various shapes, but rain-forest leaves look much alike. They are smooth and have tips from which water can drip. As raindrops fall with large resonant plops onto the broad leaves, the air feels heavy and damp, like wet sheets, but weightless.

"Seattle Six is number one," Ben advises us, and he hands round a guide to the whole family's tail markings.

Suddenly golden monkeys appear overhead, making chucking sounds and leaping from branch to branch. What a thrill to see them high and in the wild, where they belong, silhouetted by huge ferns, swinging through rays of sunlight. Instinctively, I wrap my hand around a slender tree trunk. Imagine sliding through the canopies with such grace, with such ease. At last we see Seattle Six, whom we've now begun to refer to as the Groom, his thick fluffy fur a dark chestnut gold, not the pale blond of zoo tamarins. One by one the monkeys inspect the cages and get caught—all except the Groom, who at one point reaches in carefully over the tripwire and snatches a banana.

"He's a smart little bugger," Ben says. "We're going to have all on catching him." Hours later, after we've tried rebaiting the traps, rearranging the tripwires, laying a trail of banana crumbs, we are starting to despair. Leaving Nelson in the glade, Ben, Alfie, Joleen, and I return to the pasture.

"Okay, cricket hunt!" Ben says. It's a desperate measure, but we're running out of ideas. So the four of us creep through the tall grass in search of crickets. While we're cricket hunting, we watch a cowboy on horseback pursuing three cows that have drifted into the forest. Ben jogs in and chases the cattle out; the cowboy thanks him and trots the cows downhill. Most Brazilians picture the jungle as a primitive, irrational kingdom full of specters and goblins. It is the id-like center of their country. Civilization and progress lie in the chrome meccas of the cities, in plowed land, in the future, not in the pagan and inexplicable past. They respect those who work in the forest, but think they're *maluca* (crazy) ever to sleep there.

"Got one!" Joleen yells, holding up a fat cricket. Ben pulls a piece of wire from his pocket and makes a noose around the middle of the insect. Alfie and I catch more crickets, and soon Ben has a kicking stringful, which he carries back to the glade. Tamarins can never resist a juicy squirming cricket. At last the Groom risks the trap and is caught. We carry him out of the forest, tramp back down the hill, and place him in the back of the truck, then head back to camp.

Before dinner, we process the Groom. In the wild, tamarins develop a luminous glow to their fur. He has sweet-potato-colored legs, bright yellow atop his forehead, a reddish beard and arms, and a chest and belly the tawny gold of an autumn cornfield. A thick mane framing his face makes him look like an Aztec sun god. Holding him in my hands, I feel his strange fur—soft, but also tense, like spun glass. Occasionally his eyes open; they are dark doubloons. Who could invent a creature as startling as this? Do they dream? Will images be weaving through his mind like shadows among the trees? When he wakes, he shakes his head and stumbles for a few tipsy moments. We carry him down to the Brookfield family's cage and open the door, which is laced together with three small lengths of wire.

Bits of wire are the real currency of the camp, and many people carry them tucked into a pocket or waistband. Wire secures the *comidoros,* the water dishes, and the bananas hanging in the cages; it's essential for building the *comidoros;* it latches the doors to the cages; it holds a bit of screen over the nest-box entrance to seal the monkeys in for travel; it holds freshly noosed crickets; it will fasten almost anything to anything else.

"I thought it was silver duct tape men couldn't live without," I say, as Ben drops an extra bit of wire into his pocket. Suddenly his face takes on a primal fire and he makes an ancient-ancestor hooting sound.

"*Silver duct tape!*" he says.

Beate and I laugh, in part because we are both obsessed with Ziploc bags—precious indeed in an insect-drenched environment—and we have each brought along dozens of them. The men need to hinge and join things; we need to keep things protected and intact.

"It's really annoying when gender differences are as clear as this, isn't it?" she says, running a hand through her short, strawberry-blond hair.

As the Groom enters the cage and settles on a branch, the Brookfield monkeys one by one peek out of their nest box and begin to chatter; then the female trots over to him and sits close. They feed together on bits of apple and banana. So far, so good. If they both sleep in the nest box tonight, it's a match.

Back at the house, two hard-drinking cocktail hours begin, featuring local concoctions, followed by dinner at the long table, which everyone shares, digging into pots of black beans and rice, fried squash, fresh French bread, and a mixed grill of sausage, chicken, and beef. When talk turns to open-air grills and barbecues, Ben sets down his fork and tells of his deep regard for wood.

"In the fireplace inside my house in Maryland I burn red oak, occasionally some white oak or birch for smell, and black locust if

I can get it. That's prime firewood, for heat and ambience. I don't cook there. Now, in the barbecue grill I use oak and beech, depending upon the meat and whether I want a real smoky, slow-cooked flavor or a fast, searing, hot effect. In the outside fireplace, on the back porch, I sometimes keep a big pot boiling and make things like beans or chili over an open fire, and for that I use only red oak."

"What is it about wood that you find so exciting?" I ask.

"It's something deep within me, from my soul, something primeval. I like having exactly the right wood cut in exactly the correct lengths, thicknesses, and states of dryness for the task at hand. And I love splitting wood. The nicest way is to go outside on a very cold winter day, when the water inside the wood has frozen and expanded, and when you hit the log with an ax or maul, it splits cleaner and the air resounds with the sound of the wood and you quickly work up a sweat. You can take off your shirt and soon the steam's rising off your body. It's six o'clock in the morning and dawn is just coming up. People get pissed off at me because it wakes everybody up. But that's heaven. That's bliss." Smiling at the thought of such peace, he returns to his food, buttering a thick knob of French bread.

Soon dessert and coffee appear, and people relax in armchairs or stroll out to the porch. Joleen has brought along a Portuguese-English phrase book, and, taking one of the handsome young Brazilian men aside, regales him with its risqué phrases and obscenities. "Sperm!" she says to him in Portuguese. Then, "Enlarged scrotum!" and "I'm sexually excited."

"Going to be an interesting couple of weeks," Ben says.

As darkness falls, bats pour like smoke from below the porch eaves. A thriving bat colony lives in the crawl space under the roof, and their droppings have attracted a sea of mealworms, which Fernando sometimes uses to feed monkeys that seem ill or need extra protein. Both the bats and the mealworms are welcome guests. Kitchen scraps go to feed the chickens, whose eggs we eat. Most things in camp are recycled. With a whoosh of car lights, Roberta arrives in her VW bug and joins us as dinner is finishing. This is early for her. Usually she shows up late at night, to chat and drink beer and then crawl into her top bunk fully dressed. At dawn she sets out for the day's work, taking with her the leftovers from the camp's dinner, which she will eat the next day, alone at the abandoned train station she's converted into a lab. There is something not quite earthlike about her. After two years in Brazil (almost all of that time in the wild), she talks and gestures like a Brazilian, punctuating her animated conversations with the Brazilian hand snap—five or six in quick succession. Sometimes she will begin a sentence normally but, by the end of it, slip straight into the Twilight Zone.

"I really love it here," she says, all atwitch, taking a swig of beer, "but what's starting to get to me is the glasses." We consider the small tumblers. "They're jelly jars, you know, jelly came in them. I'm sick of drinking out of jelly jars, you know where jelly was, jelly jars." Howie's, Alfie's, and my eyes find one another. "And of course, the mosquitoes," she continues. "You get into bed and they're there, they follow you, they wait, they're huge and bloodthirsty and there's no way ever to protect yourself from them when they decide to come after you." Yet I've noticed that she leaves the bedroom door open at night with the overhead light on, inviting mosquitoes in.

She is ambivalent about going home—her life, family, work, culture, now are Brazilian. But she must return to her American university to finish a Ph.D. The camp is fond of her and doesn't worry about her excessively if she's late or missing for a meal, since her unpredictability is predictable. And, in any case, she has become the forest. Soft and curvy when she first arrived, she now looks muscular, lithe and treelike. Her long hair hangs straight down her back, and her bangs are chopped short in an Indian style. Her skin has gone beyond tan to cured mahogany.

In this sort of business something always gets left behind, sometimes one's country or family. After deep immersion, some people cross the line and become so used to being independent and in the wild that they never do return, but wander, taking low-paying jobs in various projects, perhaps marrying a local. Roberta is right at that point. For two years solid she has been collecting data, vast amounts of it, about the vegetation in this forest. And now she must return to the States and make sense of it all, synthesize it, write up a dissertation, apply for jobs, return to an alien and formal world. There was a brief moment during the seventies when people with field experience could find jobs in the conservation movement. But now those who do not return to academe may find themselves suddenly in their forties, drifting, without a job at a college or a corporation, their lives all experience, no security. Suddenly weary of accumulating life, they have no way of re-entering normal society. An ecologist with invaluable time in the field, Roberta must return to a college degree and a job while she still can. One day, she will probably send graduate students of her own to Brazil.

"How was Christmas?" I ask.

"Oh, I made this great crèche—entirely out of beetles, you know, those beautiful green and blue and black beetles, all different colors and sizes. Whenever I'd find one during the year, I saved it for the crèche—the Mary beetle, the Joseph beetle, the Wise Men beetles, the sheep beetles. Ben found the Baby Jesus beetle for me—a small, really spectacular beetle. They have to be dead, of course. I've been thinking a crèche of flies would work well, too. But the beetles, man, they made a really cool crèche."

"Roberta needs to go home," Fernando says, grinning.

Sunday morning. The rain, falling thick and loud on the wide banana palm leaves, makes a thin gray screen. The screened windows create their own visual fog, so, looking out, we see two rains, one silent, both steady. At the porch worktable, we chop up bananas, apples, pineapples, peaches, and Monkey Diet; then we carry the food to each monkey cage. The monkeys eat slowly because of the rain, and we wait for them to finish. Today is release day. At the house, the others are up and busy, eating breakfast, packing a lunch. Since we may be out for many hours, we drink too much coffee, eat too many fried sugared bananas. Despite the rain, the air feels electric with excitement as we seal the monkeys into their nest boxes and carry them into the van with us.

Half an hour later, we turn off the main highway and enter "Dois Coqueiros," the Fazenda of Two Palms, with its picturesque pair of houses set against sprawling farmlands and forested hills. We drive along the muddy road until the road runs out, and then climb on foot through high forest, past a jungle waterfall, to a fig tree that has a yellow ribbon tied around its trunk. There we angle up a steeper hill to a tree with a red ribbon. Luis has already chosen this site as a fine home for the monkeys, with fruit trees all around and a nice array of branches and vines. When Ben sets down the blue-and-white nest box at the base of the tree, I see a small gold face peering out from behind the screened-over door. I think it is Jenny, the mother, who is so eager for freedom, although I can't be sure without seeing the tail markings. I wish there were some way to reassure and quiet her. She doesn't know that we're here to help her, and that all the turmoil and confusion of the past few days will soon be over.

Luis takes off his slicker and climbs twenty feet up the tree to where the thick trunk forks. With his machete, he clears an area for the nest box. Andrea tosses him pliers and a coil of wire; Ben throws him a freshly cut branch to use as a crossbar. Then Ben sends the nest box up a rope pulley and Luis wires it into place, fixing a branch close to the doorway so that the monkeys won't have far to leap.

"Monkey kindergarten," Ben says. "We're trying to make it as easy for them as possible."

The moment Luis opens the door to the nest box, Jenny rushes out. Next out is her daughter, Maria, then the male, Melvin, whom we had captured as a mate for Jenny, then the kids. These last four suddenly begin a harsh, rhythmic chatter at Mom. There's no question about its purpose. Loud and grating, it has an immediate effect—she rushes higher into the tree and looks truly rattled. The chatter grows louder and more strident. Mother falls twenty feet to the ground.

"Oh, no," I say, laying one hand up the side of my cheek, as humans so often do when distressed. My instincts beg me to help her, but I stay put.

"Should somebody follow her?" Beate asks anxiously.

"She's got a collar," Ben says. "Look, she's up again."

Climbing another tree, Mother hurries from branch to branch until she is halfway down the hill. Stoning her with their hard voices, her family continues driving her away. If she runs at speed, we'll have to follow to keep an eye on her, despite the mud and rain. Middle-aged Jenny is still vibrant, active, and fertile. She has small kids to raise. But she's a little too old to find another family elsewhere. What will become of her? It's soul-wrenching to watch her exiled from her family, discarded, banished to the prison of a far tree.

Maria sits on a branch by the nest box and makes alarm calls after her. She has temporarily won the new male, who arch-walks past her to assert dominance, then scent-marks a branch. The kids quiet down and begin scampering around the tree, eating from the *comidoro*. Not quite out of sight, Jenny begins slowly working her way back toward the family. Seeing this, Maria and Melvin go out on a limb together and yell at her a monkey version of "Don't come in, lady!" She backs away. Then they return to the top of the nest box. One of the kids makes a hoarse, ear-splitting rasp—the characteristic "infant call" that serves as an appeal to be fed. Sometimes even a fully grown adult, in moments of stress, will make the infant rasp to defuse a tense situation, saying in essence, "Don't hurt me, I'm really still an infant." But the kid does something that surprises us: he goes to the stepfather, stares him right in the face, and does the infant rasp again. The father has no food, isn't eating. "Feed me," the kid continues to plead, "feed me, feed me." In this strange new land, with his natural father missing and his mother driven away, the kid must ingratiate himself with Stepfather. The other kid scampers in, rolls over, and begs the stepfather to groom him. Stepfather begins slowly to play with both of them. As the main family quietly eats, Mother sneaks in a little closer. Seeing her, Maria leaps to the top of the nest box, taking the high ground above her male, arch-walks back and forth, and chatters aggressively. Her body language says, *That's my man!*

When Mother retreats, the kids, the stepfather, and the daughter begin exploring their new world, gamely, without much hesitation. One scratches with a hind foot, doggy-style, another wraps its whole body around a branch. Sometimes they do the splits between branches or sit back on their haunches like kangaroos. They excel at catching three branches with three of their feet and laddering up, or climbing a vine hand over hand. As addled as we are about Jenny, we're also gladdened by how well the rest of the group seems to be adjusting.

"This is a group that was used in orientation experiments back at the zoo," Ben explains. "A grad student would disorient them on purpose—move their nest box while they were sleeping so that they'd wake up in an unfamiliar place—and it really seems to have helped. I'm so excited about this."

Dealing with novelty or random change is difficult for tamarins. Facing the unknown can be overwhelming. But once change becomes habitual, novelty itself becomes a familiar state of things. Life is still awkward and demanding but not paralyzing; they learn to puzzle things out.

One of the kids tries to walk on a thin palm leaf and skids onto a branch. Ben calls a running commentary on all their movements to Andrea, who jots it down in a notebook. Mother continues to keep her distance, moving slowly among the branches of a nearby tree. That she is moving at all is a good sign. We're afraid she may stop at any moment, forfeit the battle, become helpless, give in to despair, and starve or fall to a predator.

Sitting on the forest floor, we humans vocalize to one another and swat at mosquitoes. The monkeys ignore us—we are part of the leaf litter; we are background. Sometimes they stare at us and hold our gaze for a slender moment, but the moment passes. They do not search our faces for familiar traits. They do not need to bridge the distance. They would not understand our loneliness as a species. Ben speaks in three languages: Portuguese, English, and scientific code. One moment he says, "She's driving the hussy away!" and the next, "CB-Three solicit-grooms LA-Five." The daughter is all intimidation, the mother all guile and diplomacy. The daughter stands next to the male, strikes aggressive poses at the mother, and shrieks. The mother waits till the male is alone, then approaches him seductively and asks him to groom her.

"Good ploy," I say.

Ben cautions me against crediting them with intuition. "They're like Swiss watches," he says. "They just react. Their hormones tell them what to do. They don't think about it."

He doesn't like attributing cognition or emotion to the monkeys, or calling them by name, or regarding them aesthetically. So it makes him wince when I say that the cowering mother seems "intimidated" by the daughter's display, or when I describe one of the kids as "cute."

"Look at it like this," I finally offer good-naturedly. "As a higher-primate female, I'm hardwired to respond to the young of all mammalian species as cute, especially lower primates. Think of it as part of my evolutionary program."

Ben smiles, runs an open palm over his beard, nods. "Fair enough," he says.

For hours, we watch the family feeding and playing, while Andrea carefully notes even their smallest actions. Observers are taught a complex shorthand, with which they must record many data about many individuals at once. Sometimes they also choose an animal at random and simply follow its actions for ten minutes solid. The best observer does a good "scan"—a mental snapshot of where every monkey is in time and space. Coolheaded observation is crucial to the project, which is collecting reams of data about the tamarins' habits, family life, and nutrition. But workers like Andrea are far from uninvolved.

The Golden Lion Tamarin Project is a hands-on enterprise. For ages, people have taken rare or exotic animals out of the wild and kept them in zoos. Now zoos are sending animals back into the wild. Most scientists and naturalists live by a prime directive only to observe animals, never to intrude in nature's ways, even if it means watching a favorite animal die of illness or fall to a predator. Abstinence is a central ethic among scientists, for whom "Observe but do not interfere" reigns as a strict commandment. But zookeepers are used to handling animals, doctoring them, breeding them, protecting them, and moving them around; they live by a different code.

"When I began doing business in 1970," Ben says, sitting down under the shelter of a palm leaf, "zoos were right on the cusp of change. Up to that time, zoos had largely been consumers—taking animals out of the wild in order to stock their collections. But most of the enlightened zoos recognized that it was irresponsible to go into the wild and wantonly take animals for collections. Zoos had to begin to produce self-sustaining populations of animals. It wasn't only a question of self-interest. The zoos' collections of animals were an extraordinary scientific resource for behavioral research. They also had a responsibility to encourage conservation in the wild, either by buying up and protecting reserves, or by sending experts into the field to assist researchers and wildlife managers. And they realized their tremendous obligation to educate the public. If world conservation is going to be successful, we will need to move resources from the affluent, developed countries—largely in North America, Europe, and Japan—southward into the tropics, where countries are developing. Zoos have the responsibility to teach people about biology, ecology, conservation biology, world economics."

"Is it best for animals to live in an artificial Eden?" I ask.

"Zoos need to rethink their philosophy," Ben says. "At the moment, it's to protect every individual animal and spare it stress, spare it hunger, spare it climatic extremes. We carry around with us this notion that the wild is somehow a romantic paradise, but look around you. The wild tamarins are half-starved; they're infested with parasites. They don't have veterinary care; they don't have reliable food sources; they're subjected to wet and cold; there are predators stalking them every minute. It's not paradise at all. And zoo-born animals are ill equipped to deal with these kinds of challenges. If we are to maintain selection for genetic adaptiveness to deal with such challenges, and if we are to provide experience for zoo animals that will enhance their adaptiveness, we are going to have to intentionally subject them to stress, for the sake of their species. This is going to be a real problem, because zoos are used to thinking only of protecting the individual. And visitors to zoos get to like individual animals. But, you know, conservation isn't about Bambi. We're trying to save a whole species, a whole ecosystem in which it lives."

In the palm canopy, a young male with a Don Ameche face searches for insects. Suddenly he falls, spread-eagled like a cat, and bounces on the ground thirty feet below, sniffs, grabs a low branch uncertainly, and climbs back up. Although he seems a little unsteady, he's not favoring any of his limbs. It's the first time he's been more than a few feet from the ground, and the long drop must have been quite a shock. Walking back and forth on a branch, he leaps to a tree closer to us, then sits and scans. He seems to know where he wants to go, but he's reluctant to jump onto thin, fragile branches to get there. Stepfather quickly leaps over to the stranded kid and shows him a safe route back to the nest box, and the kid follows.

"Excellent, excellent," Ben says. "Lesson one in the forest—be able to find your way home. We've sometimes had an animal sit there all day long and be unable to work it out."

Back at the nest box, the kid reaches into the *comidoro* and crams a wad of banana into his mouth until his cheeks bulge like a trumpet player's. A minute later, he holds a piece of apple in his fingers and delicately nibbles.

"In a sense," Ben says, "this biological reserve is also a zoo. It's only about twelve thousand acres. It's got gates with locks; it's got firebreaks; much of it isn't forest but the remnants of old ranches; it's got some cultivated fruit trees; it's got roads; airplanes fly overhead; trains go through it; there's a dam on one perimeter. We've got monkeys with radios on them; we've got people out studying small mammal populations at night. So it's not really very different from a zoo, is it? More and more, as we look at national parks and wildlife refuges around the world, we're finding that they need to be intensively managed if they are to survive. The best we can hope for is to save ten or fifteen percent of an ecosystem for posterity.

"This has resulted in one of the most amusing ironies in my professional life. When I got into the zoo business in 1970, there was a certain arrogance among people who studied animals in the wild. They looked with disdain on people who worked with animals in zoos. It was less real; it was less normal; it was less natural. And indeed, it is less natural. But now, twenty years later, as national parks and reserves become key refuges for wild populations, wildlife managers are facing problems that zoos have already solved. For example, if you need to move a male rhinoceros from one reserve to another to breed, because it no longer can migrate normally, you'll come to a zoo and say, 'I never moved a rhinoceros before. How do you do it? How do you get it into a crate? What sort of crate do you use?' Of course, in time, everyone will realize that it isn't necessary to move a rhinoceros at all—all you've got to do is move his semen. But meanwhile zoos have mastered many techniques of breeding and handling wild animals."

When an owl flies over, the monkeys automatically flatten them-selves against a tree. With land predators, they act differently. If a snake, ocelot, bamboo rat, or wild dog showed up, they would mob it. There's safety in numbers, as schooling fish and warring humans know, and the kids, who hang back a little, learn to rec-ognize dangerous animals.

"What are the chances for this tamarin family?" I ask.

"Over the years, we've reintroduced ninety golden lion tamarins. Thirty-five of those still survive in the wild. Some have to be fed every day. Some are totally self-sufficient. Those reintro-duced monkeys have given birth to forty-five live offspring, of which thirty-three are still alive today. And some of those have also reproduced, so we have second-generation births. For a rein-troduction program, that's about average. The record for the Ara-bian oryx in Oman, or the red wolf in the southeastern United States, or the eagle or falcon, is about the same. But success in con-servation is a posthumous wish, because we're not concerned only about what we achieve in this decade or in this century. Conserva-tion really is a timeless concept. You're conserving forever. You're conserving so that evolution can proceed naturally. I personally will never know whether the Golden Lion Tamarin Conservation Project was successful. All I can look at are short-term goals. One goal is reintroduced GLTs that are totally self-sufficient. We have several such groups now, and I would say they are wild. But I'm also glad that the golden lion tamarin has become a powerful sym-bol in Brazil, not just for the conservation of the Atlantic coastal rain forest, but for the country's wilderness in general."

Toward nightfall, Mother returns to the family and, though sub-dued, begins to feed with them. Relieved, we head back to camp. On the way out of the fazenda, we stop to say hello to the man-ager, who surprises us by explaining that he's changed his mind about the location of the monkeys. Now he would prefer that the nest box be on a different hill on the other side of the estate. Heart-sick, Ben, Beate, and Andrea try to persuade him to let the nest box stay where it is, but he's adamant, and there is little they can do. Nothing is on paper. The project relies solely on the goodwill of the landowners. But this will mean moving the family once more, and with the mother and daughter quarreling, the last thing we want to do is to shift them to another neighborhood. Also, there is the problem of the African ("killer") bees, which have already invaded one of the nest boxes on the opposite hill. Last year, Andrea and the others watched as bees stung to death a mother and her babies. When the male fell to the ground with twenty-three bee stings, Andrea grabbed him, rushed him back to camp, and gave him steroids, which saved him.

"Let's see how they're doing tomorrow," Ben says as we bounce over the muddy road, travel a few miles down the highway, and wind our way back to the main house, where we find the others going about their chores.

One quickly adapts to the routines of camp life. Because towels never dry, I get into the habit, after washing my hands, of drying them on my hair. Clothes will dry only if hung in the generator house, but then they smell strongly of diesel fumes and, by midweek, also of the possum carcass someone has hung up. Toilet paper is never flushed but tossed into a basket beside the bowl. On patrol, the best way to fight the mosquitoes is to clothe every inch of skin. When peeing in the forest, it's a good idea to wave both hands near your butt to keep the mosquitoes away. On rainy days, the mud roads grow slithery as soap, and one must always be ready to push cars out of ditches. One sweats mightily climbing in the forest, and it's easy to become dehydrated, so whenever we pass a wild fruit tree, we stop and pick papaya, jambo (a red, pearlike fruit), passionfruit, or coconut.

Dressing on the porch one morning, I find small UFOs clinging to my boots and realize that I have inadvertently become a dispenser of rain-forest seeds. A few men and women of the reintroduction team arrive with a three-toed sloth they've found, and others with baby opossums. No sooner are they gone than a large ferret with a white chevron on its forehead runs across the yard, chasing a large rodent and harassing the chickens.

"Get the rooster!" Joleen urges him, and we laugh, because the rooster has jackhammered into everyone's sleep.

Setting out at last, we head first for a hill where a tamarin family from Omaha lives. They're not at their nest box, where we leave bananas, apples, and fresh water. Putting on headphones and holding up a large aerial, we locate them to the south and set off. First we follow them across a stream into a dense swamp of bamboo, white ginger, and thorn bushes. Tall, curly-haired P.C. machetes a way through the undergrowth; then the monkeys change direction and flee uphill all the way to the top. For us, the climb is steep and muddy, with clutching vines, thorn-wrapped trees, large spiders, and stinging insects. We must orient ourselves fast as we rush from branch to branch, guessing which ones will hold our weight, which will send us tumbling into thorns. There is something wonderful about being forced to brachiate through the trees, something thrilling about climbing and leaping at ground level, as I know the tamarins are doing in the canopy. Falling is also a fear for us on so steep an incline, and every handhold may conceal a fire ant, poisonous spider, or girdle of thorns. Dashing in three dimensions isn't easy, and all of us end up skidding, sliding, slipping, revising, straining muscles, getting small scratches and bumps. Two hours later, we see the monkeys at last, quietly eating bananas in a low tree. Making a few notes, we return exhausted to the main road. There we stop to eat the sandwiches, bananas, and cookies we packed for lunch, and I take the opportunity to study the rain forest's insect parade (one reason the ground isn't a safe place for tamarins).

In Adrian Forsyth and Ken Miyata's classic *Tropical Nature*, they suggest that you "do not beat a hasty, embarrassed retreat" after nature calls "but sit quietly nearby" and watch what happens to the dung, because it will teach you much about how the rain forest works. First there will be the scarab beetles, then feeding and contesting flies. There may be as many as fifty species of dung beetle before the whole show is over. In part, they explain, this is because our dung is protein-rich, whereas the normal carnivore dung insects encounter "consists mostly of bones, feathers, and hair, and offers few rewards to diligent beetles. Bird droppings, with their high concentrations of uric acid, are savored only by a few ants and butterflies." Of course, rotting fruit does just as well in this experiment.

When we've rested, we drive to another fazenda to find Marty and the Los Angeles family. Climbing up again through dense foliage, we see Marty overhead, playing with two tawny babies.

Tumbling all over him, clinging to his back, burbling, the kids look like they're having fun, and Marty seems to be enjoying his new role as pater familias. An older female sits on a branch nearby, searching each twist of a palm leaf. She scampers to a broken tree and probes its crevices. One of the kids follows her. Reaching her arm up to the shoulder inside a branch knoll, she grabs something feisty and drags it right to the opening. The kid scurries up, and immediately she releases her grip. The kid reaches in with both hands and much effort, dragging out a cricket almost as big as he is. She must be hungry, but she sits quietly, like altruism incarnate, as her little brother devours the entire cricket, crunching loudly through its shell. Then she leaps to another branch, and little brother follows, climbing onto her back, as she joins Marty and the twins. The female buries her head in Marty's chest, asking him to groom her, which he does. She sniffs his face, rubs against his body, makes soft, cheerful, trilling sounds. For an hour, we sit contentedly watching one tableau after another as they unconsciously act out all the scenes of a happy family playing, feeding, exploring the world together. Finally, we pack up to leave.

Back at the van, we find Andrea and two men of the reintroduction team waiting with bad news. All hell has broken loose with the Columbia family. Jenny bit Maria viciously on the neck and drove her out of the nest box, thus restoring her authority and reclaiming the male. When Maria ran to the top of a hill, the family not only shunned her, they began leaving without her. So the reintroduction team captured the daughter and brought her to us.

What to do? Ben strokes his forehead hard, as if he could erase what he just heard. We all were hoping the Columbia females would stop squabbling, make peace, and get on with family planning.

"Well," he says, "it was a good try. Now what will we do with the daughter?"

Transferring Maria to our van, we head back to camp. How frightened she looks, sitting in one corner of her cage, occasionally making a long call, to which no other monkey replies. This has been a disturbing week of many journeys for her, and we're not sure what her future will be. At the moment, there aren't any families in need of a new mother. Should she be sent to the zoo in Rio?

Kept in solitary at camp in case a position in a family opens up? Neither seems a good option.

At camp, we clean out the Brookfield Zoo's old cage and put Maria in it by herself. We are a sad lot, standing in the drizzle, wondering what to do for her. One by one, we drift back to the main house to wash up and get ready for dinner. An hour later, the deputy from a Brazilian conservation agency arrives with a GLT from a nearby town. The animal had been stolen as a two-month-old and was kept in a small cage in someone's house for two years. Acting on a hot tip, the deputy went straight in and confiscated the monkey.

Ben throws his hands to heaven and thanks God in Portuguese. Ziggy is a male of breeding age—perfect for Maria. Our prayers have been answered. We process Ziggy right away. He's fat from being a pet for so long, and his calls are those of a baby. Unfortunately, he didn't have the example of adults to emulate. But he looks healthy enough. Because of Ziggy, the camp's mood brightens as cocktail hour begins. Out on the porch, Beate gives two of the Brazilians haircuts. Fernando sorts slides of trips he made to several of Brazil's national parks. Joleen flirts hard with Luis, Zique, and P.C. At a large sink, Howie scrubs dirt from his clothing with a stiff brush and a bar of soap. Alfie crosses the porch doing a high, rapid finger snap. Ben rubs his back against a corner of the building to scratch, like a cart horse, with a huge, contented smile on his face.

In the morning, the rooster crows thirty-four times in a row, pauses, phlegmily clears its throat, then continues crowing. In deep darkness, I stretch one leg over the side of the bed, sink slowly, and am relieved to feel a chair underfoot. Like a mole, I know my way blind to the kitchen, where a candle is already throwing shadows among the pots and pans hung on the walls. Alfie, the maestro of *cafèzinho*, has set water to boil; Ben is getting out canisters of dried milk and chocolate. "Bom dia," we say groggily to one another. At the sound of the screen door opening, we turn and see Fernando standing in the doorway but not entering the room. His face looks troubled.

"Your country is at war," he says anxiously.

With that news, the morning's events move fast: telling the others, borrowing a shortwave radio, clustering around it and listening to the Voice of America. It seems impossible that we are at one of the ends of the earth and yet are receiving war-zone news that's only thirty minutes old. Mainly, we all feel shell-shocked, helpless, and worried about our families. Although our adrenaline is pounding, there's nowhere to focus it. The Brazilians are sympathetic, worried both about the Gulf War itself and about their economy, which is frightfully unstable. And what will happen to the last families of tamarins? If there's a sentiment we all share, it's the one Zique expresses when he says, "The whole world is *maluca*."

Camp work still must be done. It's time to put Ziggy in with Maria, and we carry him down to her cage. Although he's two years old, and therefore should be sexually mature, he hasn't seen other tamarins before. Running right to the floor of the cage, he crawls on the wire and squeaks like a baby. Maria pokes her head out of her nest box and looks at this new teenager but doesn't seem interested. Ziggy fusses with his radio collar, finally bending the antenna right in half. He talks baby talk, trips on the branches, and crawls on the floor. Maria studies him again, harder this time, then ignores him. He doesn't sound like an adult male, or move like one, and he's fat. Somehow he's giving her all the wrong cues, and she may well be finding him the monkey equivalent of a nerd.

"Oh, brother," Beate sighs. If it isn't one thing it's another. "We were happy too soon about her."

"Well, it's not over yet," Ben says. "Maybe he'll watch her awhile, she'll watch him awhile . . . maybe . . . maybe . . ." His voice trails off.

Some of the men set out on their morning rounds while we Americans cluster round the shortwave radio on the porch. As we listen to war news, Howie paces, and Ben obsessively sweeps the porch. We are all wearing war clothes—camouflage pants, desert boots, khaki shirts—and they feel too appropriate. In one sentence, we lament Ziggy's behavior, in the next, Saddam Hussein's. They weave together effortlessly. Life is struggle. Life includes all of this—the preservation of lower primates who cannot help themselves and the monstrous acts of higher ones who are equally, but differently, out of control. The world is *maluca*. The rain begins to fall in thick, lenslike drops, with a slow-motion quiver and only the faintest drumbeat. In a storm like this you can get drenched walking a few yards. How will Ziggy and Maria be faring, we wonder. Tamarins may live in the rain forest, but heavy rain disturbs them. Putting on our ponchos, we walk down to their cage.

At first one of them seems to be missing. Has something happened to Ziggy? Maybe Maria is playing hard-to-get in the nest box. Then Ben starts to grin. It's not one monkey we're seeing but two. Ziggy and Maria are huddled together on a branch, arms wrapped tightly around each other. Fear of the storm, or chill, has sent them into each other's arms. At nightfall, when we check again, they've disappeared into the nest box.

"Another success story," Ben says, as if it had been the simplest, most worry-free process on earth.

Alfie, Howie, Ben, Beate, and I will be leaving tomorrow, but Joleen has decided to stay on in camp an extra week; she's bought one of the "dental floss" bikinis popular on the beaches of Rio, and the Brazilian men have agreed to teach her the lambada. For Andrea, Fernando, Luis, and the rest of the reintroduction team, work will continue with all its usual excitement—the fazenda owners, the African-bee attacks, the poachers, the soap-opera-like family dramas of quarrels, truces, and hardships—despite world events. What will become of the Columbia family? I wonder. Of Ziggy and Maria? Of Marty and the kids? Will they find enough food and water? Will they learn to thrive in their strange new land full of savage and nourishing trees? It is as Charles Darwin once said of this region. "The land is one great wild, untidy hothouse, made by nature for herself." The jungle is timeless, and the plight of the golden monkeys more and more urgent. Soon the newspapers are put away, the radios turned off. Thick arms of water embrace the hillsides. Despite the storm, the forest seems nearly silent. All the monkeys will be in their nests, huddled together and calm. There are no sounds of bird, mammal, or thunder—only the occasional crinkling of leaves. When the rain falls in the Mata Atlantica, it throws a blanket of quiet over everything.

THE WINTER PALACE
OF MONARCHS

❧

When I was little, growing up in a rural town in the heart of the country, I used to pursue monarch butterflies across yards and gardens. Like most children, I found them magical and otherworldly, a piece of the sun tumbling across the grass. I knew about both airplanes and birds—they made noises and skedaddled through the sky. And in my foolishness I thought flying insects held only menace. But there was something special about butterflies: they were safe, clean, colorful as Christmas wrap. They were delicate and silent and even a little acrobatic as they grazed on flowers. Fluttering madly—but moving slowly—from bloom to bloom, they looked the way my heart sometimes felt. Monarch was the first butterfly I knew by name. As I grew up, I discovered that this was true for most children. If the monarch was not a national symbol like the bald eagle, it was a powerful symbol nonetheless. Embodying nature at its most benign, it reminds us of the pageantry and innocence of childhood.

Years later, I learned of the monarchs' extraordinary migrations, and that sites where they spend the winters were vanishing to businesses, highways, and housing projects. The world would be a poorer place without butterflies. So I joined forces with Chris Nagano of the Los Angeles Museum's Monarch Project,

to help persuade California to pass legislation
protecting the monarchs. In 1987 such a law was
passed. There are many other conservation
success stories—tougher problems to solve,
bigger animals to protect, more complex
obstacles than ignorance and greed to overcome.
But it reassures me to know that a small animal,
whose "usefulness" can't be proven, can be
saved through the determined efforts of a few
people.

Christmas in Southern California. In a eucalyptus grove near Santa Barbara, the bluish leaves have a talcy-white sheen that isn't snow, and the towering trees are strung with gaudy lights. Long, thick garlands of orange and yellow sway among the branches. A warm coastal breeze puffs hard, and all at once the lights scatter, exploding in the sky like falling embers. Fire from the trees? When they rise again, my mouth opens in silent surprise. Butterflies! Thousands and thousands of butterflies.

Some of the monarchs recluster in the trees, a Canaan they've traveled staggering distances to find. Others flutter to the open field beside the ocean, sip dew from the grass with hollow proboscises that unfurl from their mouths like party favors, or drink nectar from the frilly yellow eucalyptus flowers. They smear the field with orange, and when we walk through, they fly up all around us like a cloud of shiny coins. Only Bambi is missing from this fantasia of murmuring wings and unearthly calm. Trees, field, and sky are all drenched with butterflies. How did they get here?

A hundred million monarchs migrate each year. Gliding, flapping, hitching rides on thermals like any hawk or eagle, they fly as far as four thousand miles and as high as two thousand feet, rivaling the great animal migrations of Africa, the flocking of birds across North America. Occasionally, one will be bamboozled by the jet stream and wind up in Mauritius or England. They need only water and nectar to thrive, but they are sensitive to cold and must spend the winter somewhere warm or die. So, in the fall, those west of the Rocky Mountains fly to the coast of California to cluster in select groves of eucalyptus and pine, while eastern monarchs migrate to Mexico. The routes aren't learned—it's straight genetics. The butterflies that leave the grove this spring are four or five generations removed from the ones that were here last year. They tend to choose the same, sometimes less than ideal sites, many of which are disappearing. This is why the International Union for the Conservation of Nature has listed the monarchs' migrations as the world's only "endangered phenomenon."

Each site in California is different, but together they make a single archipelago of roosts, a single winter address. One site is the elaborately landscaped front yard of an abandoned $3.5 million Santa Barbara beach house, rumbled past regularly by trains. One is a campsite in Big Sur, under the gaze of wild boars, coyotes, red-tailed hawks, whales, and wide-eyed schoolchildren. One is in back of a Pacific Grove motel, where every door is decorated with a large wooden butterfly. One is right on the highway in Pismo Beach, complete with a ranger who gives butterfly talks, and a kiosk with butterfly information and brochures. One is the front yard of a white stucco hacienda-type house in Hope Ranch, whose monarch-appreciative owner beams when they arrive, as if they were a visitation of orange angels. One is a wild, windswept outcropping at Morro Bay, where no self-respecting butterfly ought to be able to survive. One is tucked behind a Zen-inspired bridge near a small waterfall on the manicured estate of the Esalen Institute, where people go to find inner peace, self-awareness, and such experiences as the gestalt of singing, but no butterfly communing, no mapping of the monarchs' auras. One site is a few miles from the Hearst Castle, right next to the oldest store on the Central Coast. Traffic whizzes by while, high up in the eucalyptus trees, butterflies mob, happy in their wintry hideout. When John Steinbeck, in *Cannery Row,* wrote about the clouds of butterflies grown drunk on the eucalyptus flowers, he was thinking of the roosts along the Monterey Peninsula, most of which are still there. At the Natural Bridges park in Santa Cruz the rangers have built a redwood platform to view the butterflies from, and each October there is a festival, featuring a balloon-and-cake party and a concert from the "5 M Band" (Mostly Mediocre Musical Monarch Mari-

posas). On Monarch Day, the mayor officially welcomes the butterflies to Santa Cruz, local poets read their works, and a person
dubbed Monarch Man, dressed in orange and black and wearing
dangling antennae, flies down a wire from a tree into the waiting
crowd. He bursts through a paper hoop and hands out black-and-
orange taffy. When the monarchs arrive, the rangers hoist a
monarch flag on their monarch pole, and it flies for six months,
until the last monarch leaves. It's a festival jubilant as those our
ancestors staged to welcome spring or the return of the antelope.
In a typical season, sixty thousand visitors come to the Natural
Bridges site. One day in December, though it was raining heavily,
about forty thousand butterflies hung in clusters from the trees,
and visitors kept arriving for an amazing eyeful.

Pacific Grove boasts two sites and goes so far as to bill itself as
Butterfly Town, U.S.A. Many of its businesses use the word
"monarch" in their names and there is a parade each year with
schoolchildren dressed in butterfly costumes. The town is serious
about its winged visitors, which have brought in many binocular-
slung tourists. There is a five-hundred-dollar fine for "molesting a
butterfly in any way." At the Butterfly Grove Inn, behind which
stands one of the prime sites, a sign threatens butterfly molesters
with a fifteen-hundred-dollar fine. That's not official—in California, a fifteen-hundred-dollar fine applies to a felony, and going to
prison for butterfly molesting would be rare, I imagine—but the
five-hundred-dollar fine is legit. There are also signs cautioning
people near the butterflies to whisper, not to spook them or yell at
them. Butterflies don't hear sound the way vertebrates do, but they
do sense vibration. There are healthy roosts under the final
approach path to the Santa Barbara Airport, beside a clanking
highway, next to a railroad track, in the concussive racket of Big
Sur's waves. But in Pacific Grove, mum's the word around clustering monarchs.

Many sites have vanished under condominiums, business parks,
avocado ranches, horse farms, golf courses, trailer parks, and other
signs of progress. In the last few years, seven sites have been cut
down, four of them around Santa Barbara. Butterfly Lane in Santa
Barbara, next to Butterfly Beach, once boasted the most famous site

in America, but now there are expensive homes instead, and "wing" means only an additional set of rooms.

To the butterflies' defense comes the privately funded Monarch Project. Its several scores of volunteers spend the winter visiting the roosts. They tag thousands of butterflies to track how fast and how far they fly (some travel up to eighty miles a day), where else they gather to roost, and how their populations may be changing. In November 1986, the project had a tag-off and set a world record, tagging 5,874 butterflies in one day. A 10 percent return is good; the project relies on people to find monarchs in their back-yards and fields and return them to the Natural History Museum in Los Angeles, as requested on the tiny white tags the butterflies wear on their wings like badges of rank.

All week, I've been accompanying Chris Nagano on his winter rounds. Chief entomologist for the Monarch Project, Chris is a slender, mustachioed young scientist with a lively sense of wonder. He takes me to the Ellwood site in Santa Barbara, where monarchs have been monitored for the past thirty years. A cloud of butterflies drifts low through the gulley and above a bank littered with the lep-rous bark of the eucalyptus, which flakes off the trees and lies on the ground like endless rolls of papyrus. There are few crawling insects; the eucalyptus oil keeps them away. A Pacific tree frog begins a long croak that sounds like someone working the tumblers of a safe. There is an artillery of falling eucalyptus seeds, whose hard, sharp nosecones hit the soft dirt with a relentless plopping. Creaking timbers make you think someone is constantly opening and shutting a door. The pungent smell of eucalyptus fills me with memories of Mentholatum rub and childhood colds.

We must tag at least two hundred butterflies at each site for our data to be statistically useful, so Chris takes a specially designed pole with a long net at one end and extends it high into a tree, scooping about seventy-five butterflies into its cornucopia-shaped maw. Fluttering madly in the net, their wings sound like a drizzle falling on dry leaves. Chris lays his green army jacket gently over them, "so they don't get agitated," and we sit down in the sun-light, in what might be an Indonesian forest, and begin lifting the butterflies out of the net, one by squirming one.

There is an art to tagging a butterfly. First you hold the soft, trembling body in your left hand, securely, although you can feel it gently quivering. With your right hand, you separate the front and back wings as if you were sliding one playing card behind another. Then you rub off a small oval of colored scales with your thumb and forefinger, until the clear cellophane of the wing appears. Children often are taught the old wives' tale that if you touch a butterfly's wing, you'll wipe off its "flying dust" and ground it permanently. But the microscopic scales are dead, like fingernails or hair. Tagging doesn't hurt the monarchs, nor does careful handling. Onto the clear window in the wing you press one half of the sticky, stamplike tag, then fold the other half over the top of the wing and press it firmly. Next, with both hands, open the wings of the butterfly to see if it's a male or female. Males have two black dots low on their wings and scent pouches (the scent is probably to alert other males rather than to attract females). The females have no black scent pouches, but they have thicker black veins for conducting heat to the body. On a prenumbered sheet, record whether you have a male or female, and indicate its condition: a 1 means perfect, a 3, battered and worn. A flawless specimen will have a radiant blue sheen and vibrant, velvety wings of deep orange and buff, on which loud islands of color float, some blurred, some clear-edged; a frilly white spotted hem around the bottom of each wing; and a body covered in a thick, mink-colored fur.

If it's a female, check to see if it's pregnant by lifting up its soft abdomen and feeling it between thumb and forefinger. The sperm a male deposits inside a female is thick with protein and vitamins, and it feels as hard as a ball bearing. I jot down "F2V," which means I've just tagged a female virgin in average condition; other numbers indicate the capture site. It is chilly in southern California in the winter, and monarchs can't fly much if it's below 55 degrees Fahrenheit. They would rather cluster to stay warm than shiver, the way other animals do, but they will shiver if they have to. One stands quaking on a log. Chris lifts it up, places it like a fluttering gold cookie in his open mouth, and breathes warm air over its muscles. Its four tiny black feet flex, and when he tosses it into the air, it flies eagerly back to its cluster high in the tree. As it approaches, all the other butterflies flap their wings to warn it not to cover them. They need the sun. It hovers, then finds a free spot lower down, clinging with its sticky two-clawed feet. All four feet are pronged like a longshoreman's steel grapple. Lift one foot free and the other three will snag tight.

Over the hill appears a class of teenagers from Bishop, about a six-hour drive inland. They are on a biology field trip to study the creatures of the tidepools, as well as the monarch butterflies. Chris ad-libs a lecture on the insect's life cycle, noting that the black-and-white-striped caterpillar from which the adult butterfly will emerge feeds only on milkweed, which contains a heart-stopping poison favored by assassins in ancient Rome. In turn the butterfly's body will carry enough poison to sicken a hungry bird. He shows them a butterfly with a beak-shaped bit of wing missing; the butterfly can still fly, and the bird will have learned not to attack others of that color and pattern. Indeed, the viceroy butterfly, though it is not poisonous to birds at all, mimics the monarch's color as a defensive sleight-of-hand.

A couple of the boys pass a football back and forth, but most of the students are rapt. Chris urges them to try their hands at tagging.

"Oh, he's so mushy!" a girl squeals as she lifts one up. Instead of rubbing with her fingers, she pulls her long red fingernails across the scales, which doesn't make the job any easier. When the butterfly flails its threadlike legs, she squeals again but doesn't let go. "Do they bite?"

Chris explains that they don't, can't, are completely harmless, hunt nothing, hurt no one, but are "pretty tough bugs" nonetheless.

She rubs a perfect window into its wing, sticks on the first half of the tag, then folds the next half over. "His antenna's caught under the tag!" Chris lifts it free, checks the sex. Female.

"Number 478 is a female." He jots in his notebook.

Grinning, the girl tosses it high into the air like a fighter pilot launched from an ejection seat.

Classes seem to be attracted to Chris when he's tagging. It can take a long time to allow a whole class to handle butterflies, but one day when an environmental issue comes up they'll remember. It's hard to learn about animals if you only see them dead on dissecting trays.

At Pismo Beach, up the coast, a park ranger comes by with a class of preschoolers on a butterfly tour. It is a brilliantly sunny day, and the butterflies are busy running their errands. Some arch their wings wide like solar collectors and sit in the direct sun. Some cluster high in the trees. Some sip dew from the grass (though they must be careful of the yellow jackets on patrol under the trees, looking for injured monarchs to kill and eat). Some collect nectar among the wildflowers. Some mate. Monarchs don't go in much for courtship. The male yanks the female right out of the air, hurls her to the ground, and attaches himself. Then, still attached, he flies off, with her dangling below, wings closed, as if she were a tan purse he was carrying, or he were returning a dropped hanky.

Seated on the fragrant floor of the eucalyptus grove, where insects are scarce and the ground is covered with the succulentlike South African ice plant (one of the few that can bear the heavy eucalyptus oils), we settle down to serious tagging. I deliver the kiss of life to each one, to warm its muscles, before flinging it back into the sky like a piece of solid confetti. Sometimes their faces are smeared with yellow grains of pollen. They all differ in shape, coloring, personality. Though many butterflies live only one day, overwintering monarchs live six to nine months. After tagging the first hundred, my fingertips are coated yellow-orange from the scales.

On my last night in California, after a week of tagging thousands of monarchs, I stop brushing my teeth when I hear a commotion in my motel room. There is a fireplace in my room at the Butterfly Grove Inn, and a wayward monarch has apparently flown down the flue. In a panic, it careers around the ceiling. I open the door to the porch. At last it settles on the warm lampshade and I grab it by the wings and carry it outside, hoping it will find its way home in the dark. The next morning I awake to such a screeching and scratching that I leap out of bed and rush to the porch. A blue jay, pacing angrily on the railing, screeches as it cocks its head toward the floor. There stands a monarch, shivering and stunned, with a beak-shaped wedge bitten out of one wing. Because I'm not awake enough to know better, I make a fist and lunge toward the blue jay to punch it in the chest. But before my hand can touch its feathers it disappears straight up. Gently, I pick up the monarch, check the wing. Not a bad injury really; it could fly. I open its wings to have a better look at it. A female. Not pregnant. I haven't any tags with me, or I would tag it. Instead, I walk across the yard with her, to where thousands are clustered high in the trees; I blow warm air over her muscles and toss her into the air. After free-falling a moment, she discovers that she's airworthy and flies up to her clan, some of whom are planing across the sky.

It's easy to get mesmerized watching the monarchs glide overhead, with the sun shining through their wings, as if they were small rooms in which the light had been turned on. A cluster trembles on a branch; then, in a silent explosion, they burst into the air and fly down to a Christmas pine in the direct sun near the road. Sitting on the tips of the branches with their wings spread wide, they might be orange and gold ornaments. They are silent, beautiful, fragile; they are harmless and clean; they are determined; they are graceful; they stalk nothing; they are ingenious chemists; they are a symbol of innocence; they are the first butterfly we learn to call by name. Like the imagination, they dart from one sunlit spot to another. To the Mexicans, who call them *las palomas,* they are the souls of children who died during the past year, fluttering on their way to heaven.

/

INSECT LOVE

Yet let me flap this bug with gilded wings,
This painted child of dirt, that stinks and stings;
Whose buzz the witty and the fair annoys,
Yet wit ne'er tastes, and beauty ne'er enjoys.

      —Alexander Pope

There are only two seasons in Ithaca, and both of them are wet: hot wet and cold wet. In August, part of the hot wet season, caterpillars suck the life from rose leaves, prenuptial ants grow wings and take to the air, armadas of tanklike sow bugs pour across the patio, hypodermic sphinx moths sip nectar from the phlox, monarch butterflies, mating in midair, look like an invisible magician's card trick, and countless other insects swarm in, under, atop, and through the grass, invade the house beams, or patrol the sky.

On such a hot, steamy evening, I decide to join an entomologist friend, Thomas Eisner, in his laboratory at Cornell University. Some people travel to the ends of the earth to discover the exotic, that ever-receding land that adds so much to life's cartography, but what I've always liked about Tom is that he ushers the exotic into his daily life. He can find it on a doorstep, at a golf course, in an abandoned lot, beneath a derelict building, along an air-conditioned hallway. Blessed by an elastic curiosity that stretches, changes shape, and snaps back like a thick rubber band, he is—in the very best sense—distractable. It's not unusual to hear that he's away in an unkempt field because some fascinating animal has kidnapped his attention.

At times he can be candid about his gift for "discovering things" (over the years, his work has been featured on the cover of *Science* more often than anyone else's), but he can also be almost masochistically modest, presenting himself as only a bit player in the high drama of life. Yet by worldwide proclamation he is "the father of chemical ecology," a field of study devoted to the chemical relationships among all living things. Not only does he see the forest for the trees, he knows how insects see that forest, too, and how the trees, looking back, flirt with and seduce the insects into ingenious liaisons. He knows how insects communicate with one another through the chemical calling cards we name pheromones. We're indebted to him for much of our understanding of insect defenses and courtship. He and his research partner, chemist Jerrold Meinwald, have made many practical discoveries, too, including nerve drugs in millipedes, cockroach repellent in an endangered mint plant, heart drugs in fireflies, and how the dangerous aphrodisiac "Spanish fly" works.

On the fourth floor of Mudd Hall, a large brick building in midcampus, sits Eisner's laboratory. I enter the office of his secretary, above whose door hangs a glass business sign: CORNELL BEAUTY SHOP. It's wired so that a wolf whistle will turn it on. Then I walk left through the door to his private office, above which a printed sign says: COME RIGHT IN, WE'RE CLOSED. On his desk sit many framed photographs of his wife of over forty years, Maria (also an entomologist), their three daughters, and their six grandchildren. At eye level on the wall, a plaque from his artist daughter credits him with being a "BioAstrology Destiny Reform Specialist," which she thought sounded more like her dad than "entomologist." The walls are a mosaic of compelling twenty-by-twenty-inch photographs he took through a microscope. At first they seem to be complex, colorful abstract designs, but each one shows an insect caught in an extraordinary behavior. There is a bola spider, for instance, holding what looks like a yo-yo at the bottom of a silk thread. The spider spins the bola around, lariat-style, and hurls it to capture its prey. Right at the end of the gallery is his prize: an enlarged photograph of a bombardier beetle in the act of zapping a foe. At the tip of its abdomen, a gun turret fires a jet of scalding chemicals. Harmless when stored separately, the chemicals combine in a special gland and become volatile as nerve gas. A master of defense and weaponry, the bombardier can swivel its gun turret, aim straight at an intruder, and fire a twenty-six-mile-per-hour blast of searing irritants, not in a continuous stream, but as a salvo of minute explosions. This "pulsed jet" is oddly similar to the propulsion system used in the German V-1 buzz bombs of World War II.

Through the next doorway I see Tom, standing pensively at a lab table, looking down into two shallow plastic bins of the sort one might find in a pantry. Tall, wiry, he has a face with many planes and inclines. One can imagine a fly rappelling down his cheekbones. He has blue eyes and wears glasses. Combed back close, his dark hair gives him a Latino flavor. In his twenties he actually wore an El Greco beard and mustache, but now there are few visible traces of the adolescence he spent in Uruguay. I don't know another scientist who has a Steinway piano in his lab—or, for that matter, a poster of Marilyn Monroe wearing black fishnet stockings and a Merry Widow bustier from which her ample bosoms seem to be tumbling.

"Come on in!" Tom calls when he sees me. He takes my hand in a strong handshake, then wraps his other large hand on top of that and squeezes. "I've been working with some of my favorite bugs—bombardier beetles." He leads me to the two plastic bins, filled with damp sand and small aluminum-foil tents splattered with beetle excrement. The tiny encampment looks still. As I bend down for a closer look, a nose-twitching whiff of something like semi-decayed duck sauce hits me.

"Where are they?" I ask.

He smiles and lifts up the silver tents. Dozens of beetles swarm over one another and dart into the corners. Blue-backed, each has a tawny plump belly, a tiny head and thorax the brown of a Stradivarius, two long antennae, and six many-jointed black legs.

"Want to hear them fire?" he asks cheerfully. I nod yes. "Okay, just reach into a mass of them and press on one a little."

"All right," I say slowly, leaning closer to one of the bins. For a minute or two, I stand frozen to the spot, eyes glued to the insects. Catching my breath, I realize that I've been twisting the bottom of my black cotton sundress into a large knot, as if I were wringing it out. Tom touches my arm reassuringly.

"Take your time," he says softly.

Raising my index finger, I direct it by willpower to move horizontally just above the bin, and vertically down an invisible elevator shaft to the damp sand. Minutes pass. Then, sliding my finger toward a crowd of beetles, I feel their legs and antennae brush my skin lightly. My right eye automatically squints tight. Another minute passes. At last I lift my finger and press it into a bunch of beetles, and *pop!*, one fires a shot. Startled, I jump back, laugh, reach in nervously and press another button-shaped back, hear another beetle fire, reach in again—this time eagerly. I've triggered the artillery, and now my index finger has three brown stains on it—the stigmata of the beetle handler—arranged like two small eyes and a mouth. Smiling at the impromptu finger puppet, I remember being eleven, rapturously watching "Mr. Wizard" on TV, and yearning to muck about in his lab. My index finger has browned like the exposed flesh of a freshly bitten apple. Bombardier beetles carry quinone in their saddlebags—an aromatic compound found in antibiotics and some plants (such as stinkweed), and used by humans for making dyes, tanning leather, and processing film. In fact, the bombardier is a diabolist with light. A desert dweller with a dark body, it lives on light-colored sand and, when threatened, splashes the intruder with its equivalent of Mace.

Because the bombardier possesses the only jet engine recorded in an animal, insect fanciers are especially fascinated by its engineering. To squirt, it pulses at a rate of five hundred to one thousand times per second. No muscle could move that fast. Instead, a passive oscillator guides the necessary chemicals into a reaction chamber, where they mix, causing a small explosion, which geysers the liquid up and out of a nozzle and at the same time closes the vent that fed liquid into the chamber. After the firing, the pressure is relaxed, the vent opens, and more liquid enters the chamber. In this way, the beetle rearms.

Bombardier beetles have a very high defense budget. It takes a lot of food to fuel such weaponry. So the beetle must forage very effectively, which means it's bound to lead a stressful existence, hunting without much concern for safety. Of course, it can afford to do that because it's so well protected. So here we have the classic vicious circle of the weaponeer: feverish hunting for resources to keep the defenses strong to enable it to be feverish.

"Let's see how they fire," I say.

"Great!" Tom answers, in a tone of voice that usually goes with gleeful rubbing of the hands.

We take a pan from the sink, wet it with iodine, starch, and a little hydrochloric acid, and place a piece of filter paper on top. Carrying it back to the lab table, Tom sets it down near an alcohol burner and arranges a small metal girder low over the paper. When he asks me to choose a "good-tempered" beetle from the sand pits, by which he means one that's reasonably docile but not ill, I make several halfhearted pounces. At last I sneak up on one, corralling it between thumb and forefinger. But darting and swerving are its forte, and it wriggles free, runs up my arm, spins around inside my elbow, and races toward the wrist. Catching it with my free hand, I hold it gently by the rim, as if it were a gem I was about to set into a bevel. My eyes wrinkle again as it tickles me with its legs. There is nothing to itch. It's just that it's making such fine nerves dance in my fingers. I can feel its mandibles gnawing at me, but they are far too tiny to break the skin. These new sensations are more delicate than any I have known with animals, and it takes a few Zen-like minutes to divine what barely detectable pressure will hold a beetle secure without pinching or crushing it. At this level, where all the sensations are new, I find it best to let my senses teach themselves. Soon I get the delicate knack of handling the fast, vulnerable, and small, and I turn the beetle around, exposing its rump. Then I melt a little wax over a flame so pure it looks colorless, drop a warm ball of wax onto the beetle's shell, and attach it to the aluminum girder. Lowering the beetle until its legs touch the paper, I let it rest there a moment. Then I take a pair of watchmaker's forceps, reach for its left rear leg, and lightly pinch the thigh. *Pop!* Out of a tiny cloud of smoke streaks a splatter of chemicals. Next, I pinch the thigh on its right front leg and *pop!*, it shoots fast in the opposite direction, leaving another telltale trail. Its accuracy is amazing, as is its ability to reload and fire within milliseconds. The noise isn't quite the sound of a cork popping, but damper and lower pitched, "like a gunshot behind a wall," Tom says, and I trust this description. His early years were filled with the unforgettable sounds of gunfire, and with uniforms and Nazis.

"Berlin in the thirties must have been frightening," I say as I reach for another leg. "Your father was Jewish?"

"Yes. A chemist. My mother a painter. And let me tell you, in the twenties, they found the Berlin of Kandinsky, Klee, and Reinhardt an exciting place. There were four different opera houses. My mother, an extraordinarily beautiful woman, rejoiced in her creativity. If she didn't have any art, she would pick up stones and make things out of them, or pick up shells. She always saw the way things could be converted into something artistic. My father was a chemist, all right, but his hobby was making perfume. I remember he made a very good imitation of 4711 cologne, and a violet perfume for my mother. But he also made mouthwash, tooth powder, a first-aid ointment, all sorts of smells and lotions. As a chemist, he was more of a theoretician than anything. His Ph.D. thesis was "How to Get Gold out of Seawater." Can you imagine? I mean, this was Germany's effort to pay the Versailles debt, and it was a classified project. Anyway, his job was to see if it was feasible to make gold out of seawater. The answer was no, but he traveled throughout the world, sampling seawater and doing extractions. And then, in the pharmaceutical business, he became involved with producing tonics, a tanning agent, curative ointments for cuts and sores, chewable vitamins for kids (much later, when he moved the family to the United States, he took out a patent for chewable vitamins)."

By now, the indicator paper is covered with what looks like a compass rose, with the tethered beetle at its center. Once more I touch a leg, and tiny droplets of spray arc over the paper. This time there's a *click-clack* (rather than the usual puff or uncorking sound) from the insect's repeatedly rapid firing.

As we gently unstick the beetle and return it to its bin, Tom looks distracted by memory. "What an exciting era my parents lived in," he says. "Society was a free-for-all. Recovering from the revolution, Berlin enjoyed the sort of chaos that has a way of bringing out the original in people, because anything that's organized is unappealing. There were hundreds of different political organizations, all struggling for identity, and a great fever to be individual, to be unusual."

"It must have been hard for them to leave."

"Hitler came in in early April, and we left at the end of April. I was not quite three, my sister six. Off we went to Spain, with nothing, a couple of suitcases. My father went from one pharmaceutical company to the next looking for a job. At last he found one, and we rented a house in Barcelona. I can still remember Julia, a wonderful maid with a big bosom on which I used to rest my head.

I just loved that, not knowing that this was the beginning of discovering sexuality. She must have been in her late twenties, a tremendous flirt. The policemen with their ornate helmets used to stop by outside, and she would flirt with them through the iron grille in the windows. She smelled like lavender, and would sneak me chocolate and other treasures.

"Then the Spanish Civil War came. Those are really traumatic memories. One day when I was seven, I was sitting in the sandbox and heard an incredible noise—a series of explosions. They were taking streetcars and filling them with dynamite and rolling them down the hill. Some apartment buildings and churches were burning. I flew out of the sandbox and ran from the racket. Suddenly Spain blew up. The Spaniards, who are capable of the greatest expressions of human warmth, can also inflict the most horrendous tortures on one another. There were so many factions at the time that it was dangerous to go out. If you made the wrong salute to the wrong truck or boat, you were in trouble. You had to know the Communist salute, the anarchist salute, and so forth. I was too old by then to see any romance in all the commotion; I was terrified. We fled Spain on a freighter, which was full of cattle infected with sleeping sickness. Mutilated nuns were on board. The boat was crammed with people, and my sister and I slept covered up by half a dozen fox terriers inside the coiled anchor chain. We only sailed for one day, but that's a long time to children. We thought it was a great adventure. Then we got to Marseilles and stayed with friends. We did some crazy things, like smuggling in other children. The world was in so much turmoil. It was total confusion. Finally, we got to Paris and found an apartment. My father rented a piano, which was a great source of strength."

"Was he a good pianist?"

"Well, he was an *enthusiastic* pianist. I started taking piano lessons, which I loved. But we didn't stay in Paris long, only about half a year. I remember how, in school, the other kids called me a dirty Nazi because I was a German refugee. We could smell World War Two. So we decided to head for South America, where my father felt he could start from scratch. But it wasn't easy to get a visa; my father and I went to the Brazilian consulate every day and lined up with hundreds of people. One day lightning struck the building next door. There was a tremendous crash, and I started screaming at the top of my lungs. I was the only kid there. A door opened—one of those doors that everyone was praying would open for them—and a man came out and asked why I was crying. My father told him about the lightning. The man sat me on his knee and patted me and told me not to cry. My father explained that we were urgently trying to get to South America, and the man felt sympathy for us and gave us a visa. Life was that sort of lottery. So we went to Brazil and, with further complications, made our way to Uruguay."

Tom stayed in Uruguay from the age of seven until he was seventeen, ten crucial years, during which he discovered puberty and Brahms. Then the family moved yet again, this time to the United States. One key to his nature may be that he's an immigrant, driven by the need to find a place for himself, a sense of address. Seeking identity, immigrants often lead a split life—trying to succeed in what is for them a more forbidding environment than it is for the native, but also drawing upon an alien childhood, whose experiences were formative. Camus once said that the whole of a person's artistic expression is the attempt to recapture through art those two or three images in the presence of which his soul first opened.

As he removes the beetle, it touches the paper and leaves a mark resembling the Chinese character for "evening." When bombardier beetles fire, they aim at the body part being pestered and invariably bathe themselves in poison. Why don't they suffer from it? Scientists don't know. Another bombardier beetle, dosed by mistake, will run off but not be hurt.

"How many times can he fire?" I ask.

"Oh, twenty or thirty. Then it takes a couple of days to reload a fifth of that."

"What happens in the meantime?" I have visions of a besieged beetle suddenly discovering its revolver is empty.

"It's in trouble. But one of the great things about bombardiers is that they rarely have to shoot in succession. The first discharge coats them with chemical, and it's repellent. I've run experiments, for example, where I put bombardiers together, let them bathe in their own defensive secretions, and then put them in a swarm of ants. The ants moved around them, but avoided touching them."

Although it may be a little odd to think of it as a form of armor, smell plays many crucial roles in an insect's life. It's similar to a telephone wire over which different kinds of messages can flow: threat, invitation, courtship; the whereabouts of food; a call to arms; a password; a death knell; the trail home.

"Why do they have such long necks?"

"That's not a neck," Tom says. "Actually, it's part of the thorax. All insects have a simple body structure, and this beetle is no exception. Let me give you the two-bit tour of an insect. First of all, insects are bilaterally symmetrical—that is, they have the same number of legs, eyes, et cetera, on each side. What does that tell us? That they move in one direction. If you had to design such an animal, where would you put the sense receptors? Obviously, on the body part that meets the conditions first. So the eyes, mouth, and antennae are all on the head. Then you've got the thorax, which is little more than a box of muscles, nothing, really, but a motor for the appendages. The gut runs through the thorax, weaving among the muscles. The wings are also on the thorax—and, by the way, these beetles are good fliers. The abdomen is this large area here," he says, running his fingertip over the widest part of the beetle. "An abdomen in a beetle—and in ourselves—is a part of the body that's unencumbered by appendages and therefore can undergo a certain amount of distention. It needs to house the expanding gonads, fertile eggs, testes, sperm packages, as well as to engorge with food. So that's the insect design. Very successful. With that combination of brain, gut, and gonads, what have you got?" He pauses dramatically. "Either an insect or the average male."

Life's theater appeals to Tom, who has a rare talent for finding a story and telling it. If you are a human physiologist, there are just so many topics to explore, just so many glands, just so many nerve centers, just so many things that can go wrong with the human body. Your focus will be relatively narrow. But, if you are one of the few researchers traveling across the almost unlimited wilderness of insect diversity—tens of millions of species, the great majority of which do not even have a scientific name—you tend to move from one pinpoint puzzle to another.

"The way Tom works," his best friend, E. O. Wilson, said one day when we sat in his office at Harvard, eating shards of Rainforest Crunch, "is that he goes into the field, sees an interesting-looking insect, or a familiar insect doing something unusual, and studies it with a wide range of paraphernalia—cameras, preliminary chemical tests, observation chambers—and finds out what it's doing, why it's unusual, where it fits in. He develops it as a story; he brings it back to the laboratory." As a renowned ant specialist and the father of sociobiology—a field that explores the biological basis for social customs, mores, and habits—Wilson knows intimately what it takes to prevail in science. "Then he turns to a collaborator in chemistry who can work out the natural-products chemistry of that species—Tom grasped years ago that most of what insects do is chemical. They communicate chemically, they defend themselves chemically—they are magnificent chemical factories. In this way, Tom treats his subjects not just as visible objects with fascinating behaviors but as chemical wonders."

Once an insect yields its secret, Tom is likely to move on to the next mystery. Because there are only a handful of investigators with his drive and ability exploring the hordes of insect species that exist, that is probably a good strategy. You'd think this would continue indefinitely, that in a Borgesian way he would move through an infinite library of stories and at the end hold the same small lamp he started out with. But over the years what he learned formed patterns and he began to tie the stories together, producing some of the first principles of chemical ecology.

"The result of all of this," Wilson said thoughtfully, "is that Tom is a pointillist. He's a person who daubs points of light on a broad canvas, which at first seems to be a random splattering of bright pigment but, as more and more pieces fill in, reveals an extremely interesting picture of a little-known part of the living world."

It is nearly ten o'clock when we finish with the bombardier beetles, put them back under their silver tents, and lock the lab up for the night. When we step outside into the dark, we instinctively turn and look back at the building, still, for once, and other-worldly in its carapace of light.

Packing for a trip to the Florida scrublands, a unique and endan-gered habitat where rare insects dwell, I let my thoughts wander over "biodiversity," a notion that dominates Eisner's life and career. Like many environmentalists, including his friend Wilson, he has evolved a bold insight about the biological future of the planet. What it boils down to is a living kaleidoscope, in which all the pieces can change and link up in many different ways. Why does biodiversity have so much to do with insects? Most people aren't much concerned about ants and flies and may even think the world would be improved if more insects went extinct. But insects aerate the soil, clean up decay, help in pollination, produce foods for us (such as honey), and teach us about genetics and chemistry. A gene is a terrible thing to waste. Remedial creation isn't possible. So we need the malaria mosquito, the voracious sand flea, the Lyme tick, and all their cousins.

It's hard for Tom to explain the concept of biodiversity to peo-ple, let alone the important role that insects play. One strategy that seems to work well is to appeal to plain, old-fashioned human greed. Drug companies help protect some rain forests because of the medicinal plants there; but Tom has begun proving that there are medicinal insects, too. Obsessed with sex, poison, and death, insects live like lilliputian Lucrezia Borgias and Machiavellis, wielding sophisticated weapons, concocting lethal potions, refin-ing aphrodisiacs. Their scourge or weaponry sometimes works as a tonic for us. As a direct result of Tom's work, Merck and Com-pany has agreed to protect the rich Costa Rican rain forest for "chemical prospecting"—a conservation coup. Of course, he first has to prove that there's an orient of treasures to be found among insects. Much of Tom's voyaging to the land of the small takes place at Archbold Biological Station, near Lake Placid in South Central Florida. I decide to join him on his annual pilgrimage, and fly down to Fort Myers one clear cold day in February.

After driving two hours northeast, past one-story towns with romantic names—Venus, La Belle, Arcadia—I turn at the Arch-bold Station sign and drive down a gauntlet of trees to a large clearing. There I find a main building, which houses a dining hall, two dormitories, a suite of lounges and offices, and four research laboratories. A huge straggler fig covers the walls, framing the doors and windows. The brick and glass are only temporary, it implies; soon enough everything will return to nature. Flanked by a grass-tufted tennis court and a garage filled with Land Rovers, the main building faces a semicircle of cottages tucked in the woods. At the office, a secretary points me in the direction of the Eisners' cottage—Number 2, next to the watertower—and I soon see it, surrounded by pink azalea bushes. Two bicycles (one male, one female) nestle together under one of the gray-and-white, wasp-patrolled awnings. Organ music pours across the screened porch. I let myself in and find Tom in the parlor, sitting at an electronic keyboard, playing Bach's Toccata and Fugue in F Major, with Maria poised beside him, turning the pages. A slender woman with short hair, large blue eyes, and delicate skin, she is wearing a pink-checked shirt and khaki trousers. Spotting me at the door, she touches Tom lightly on the shoulder, but it's enough to startle him from his reverie. His hands pause over the keys for a moment as he returns from a different world. Then we greet one another and swap news about friends. They show me the latest snapshots of their children and grandchildren and give me a glimpse of their cottage, the whole back half of which is a laboratory dominated by high-power microscopes, a hive of vials, and insect and plant specimens. Tom usually takes an evening walk, since many insects become active at night, and I decide to join him. A flashlight on a headband frees the hands for work; looking like coal miners or spelunkers, we set out to stroll through the caverns of twilight.

The evening is full of chirping crickets and the occasional saxophone melody of a bird. But humans are poor connoisseurs of insect song, which can be too high, too fast, too percussive for us to hear. It helps a little to picture how a cricket "sings," by moving a file on one wing over a ridged scraper on the other. It's similar to a guiro, the serrated gourd scraped with a stick that one finds in a mariachi band. "The poetry of earth is never dead," John Keats begins one of his loveliest sonnets, referring to the sounds made by cricket and grasshopper. Although crickets have several songs, the loudest and longest are made by randy males hoping to mate. Surrounded by the sexual yearning of countless crickets, we stroll down a sandy road, under a full, mother-of-pearl-colored moon. When darkness falls, the woods feel closer, and in the absence of reassuring cues, the mind endows the shadows with menace: rattlesnakes, scorpions, wild boars. A fast *whoosh-plod-whoosh-plod* off to our left is probably one of the white-tailed deer that share the station. My flashlight beam picks up deep cloven-hoof tracks in the sand, and we follow them a short way, until they disappear in the brush. It's a little like surgery, walking through the night world, assuming what must be where, using instruments to help feel your way along. A green star blinks in a tree.

"There's a firefly!" Tom calls, and he stalks it slowly, pouncing at the last moment to cage it in his hand.

"Have a look," he says, handing the insect to me.

Holding its wings between my thumb and forefinger, I inspect the small lantern of its body, flashing a cold green light. It looks like the sight pilots long for late at night: the green rotating beacon of an airport. I slip the firefly into a small white-capped vial. It stops flashing. I tap the vial. It flashes again.

"See, the flashing is a defensive thing," Tom explains. "It produces one of the brightest cold lights ever devised. You can read by it."

A scintillation catches my eye and I turn to see a swarm of lights in a nearby tree. If we were looking at the sky through a telescope, it would be easy to confuse the firefly-bedecked tree with a glimpse of the Beehive nebula. Watching fireflies is one of the treats of summer nights. Because we're not dark-adapted, they seem quite bright to us, but photographs barely catch a trace of them. Tom tells me that once, filming with the BBC, he gathered a whole mess of fireflies and threw them at a huge spiderweb (after he'd taken out the spider), and the cameraman filmed that spectacular cloud of fireflies. Children often share a sense of magic about fireflies. I've seen firefly auroras on my own front lawn in June. Eighteenth-century American women used to tie fireflies in their hair as decoration. I don't know what they used as a tether. Sometimes we call them lightning bugs. Glow worms are the wingless ones that keep to the ground. But they're all beetles belonging to the order Lampyridae, which have enchanted people of many countries. The ancient Chinese and Japanese both had firefly celebrations; Aristotle and Pliny described their habits. What songs would Solomon have sung to his beloved about her eyes flashing like fireflies? Because they're not mentioned in the Koran, the Bible, or the Talmud, it's probably safe to assume fireflies couldn't survive in the Near East. But the story goes that they averted a war in Cuba: When the British generals Sir Robert Dudley and Sir James Cavendish arrived off Cuba, they saw what they thought to be the torches of belligerent Spaniards onshore. So they sailed to Jamaica instead.

Fireflies flash by mixing two hypergolic chemicals. Unremarkable by themselves, these stuffs combine with a poetic flourish to build powerful, strange new substances. Nitrous oxide and glycerin, for example, produce the explosive nitroglycerin. In fireflies, the match includes luciferin and luciferase, and when they mix in the light organ under the firefly's abdomen, they give off a yellowish-green light. We're used to thinking of light sources as radiating heat, but these don't. Actually, what they shed is oxygen, too much of which living things find as toxic as too little. Manufacturers have begun to take advantage of firefly dynamics by creating beacons, for trick-or-treaters or stranded motorists, which begin to glow when you mix the two chemicals together.

"How can they do it so quickly—mix up those little beacons?" I ask.

"How can you start a heartbeat suddenly? It's amazing it was all done in six days, wasn't it?" Tom says, with a wink in his voice.

"Everything fun happened on the afternoon of the third day," I reply. "Before that it was mainly darkness and light, afterwards bureaucracy."

"Good scientific method! If you're going to have an important experiment, you don't wait until the last day or you could screw the whole thing up. . . . Hey! Just look at that flash. Isn't it wonderful!"

For some time now, Tom's been studying the "femme fatale fireflies," in work he and his graduate student James Lloyd have made famous. As it turns out, males and females flash either when they're hungry or when they want sex. In the flash-as-semaphore-of-lust scenario, the female waits on the ground or in the vegetation as she is barnstormed by a male. The male usually swoops down, and flashes for half a second while rising like a paintbrush stroke to make a *J* of light. If it's his female, she'll reply with a half-second flash. Then he'll fly to her again and swoop-flash; she'll flash back. What makes the luminous dance unique for the mates is the pause between the flashes. It's as if the fireflies were reading the rests in a visual concerto. When they're both reassured by this Morse code, they'll mate. But some fireflies are femme fatales that lure other females' mates by mimicking their flash code. When a male dives down, expecting to mate, the femme fatale eats him, not just from hunger or because she has a devilish streak, but because certain males carry defensive chemicals in their bodies. By eating such a male, the female saturates herself with a chemical armor that makes her distasteful to birds, spiders, and other predators. There's enough heart stimulant in ten fireflies to kill a human being. So, armed and dangerous, mates rely on visual passwords during courtship. Everything is at stake. Because it takes a lot of energy to flash, they personalize the pause. What we see is a night decorated with their detailed yearnings and hesitations, a small opera in light.

Elsewhere in the world—near rivers in Borneo and Thailand, for instance—there are "firefly trees" swarming with males that flash in unison to attract females from the forest. Along those midways, schooled in the neon of desire, females come to look for mates in the green-light district.

"Have you seen the firefly trees?" I ask.

"No, but I'm told they're magical," Tom says. "Isn't it interesting how fireflies vary their courtship techniques? Different human cultures develop different traditions. The same thing is true with fireflies."

"You'd think the twinkling stars would confuse them."

"Their eyesight isn't that good. Human settlements bother them, though—the air is different, the noise level, the lighting. There's really very little human activity that's compatible with the rest of the world," he says with a sigh.

I'm glad the dusk hides my slow smile. After all, Tom and Maria have raised three children and lived very much in civilization. I have as well. Part of the irony of environmentalism is questing for solutions when you know you're part of the problem.

The firefly in my hands flashes green with an afterglow of yellow.

"I'll tell you something that really blows my mind," Tom says. "Nobody knows the life cycle of the common firefly."

"Why not?"

"Because nobody knows where the larvae hang out. Can you imagine that? One of the most familiar insects in the world, and yet we're still in the dark about it."

As we stroll back to camp, small eyes peer at us from the vegetation. Some animals have a mirrorlike membrane in their eyes that reflects light. If you aim a flashlight at the woods, you can often "shine" their eyes. This works with alligators as well as with spiders. Alligator eyes shine red, like two glowing cigarette butts; many spider eyes shine green. There are guidebooks to animal tracks, and even waterproof guides to reef dwellers, which you can take skin-diving with you, but I don't know of any night guides to animal eyes.

"Shining spiders" is a favorite pastime of night-prowling naturalists. Once, at an arts center on the east coast of Florida, attracted by eye shine, I found a six-by-ten-foot spiderweb stretching from my cottage roof to the porch steps. Its maker, a fawn-colored wolf spider, large as my fist, would take the web down each morning and reweave it each evening. She always left the guy wires in place, and spun slowly across the web like a hand moving over an autoharp. I named her Anna the Aranha, and often watched her build that gossamer radar net. When it was finished she would wait in a high corner, her green eyes shining, and when something vibrated the web, she knew just where to pounce. By night, the moon walked her silk; by day, the wind made it hum.

Tom and I share a fondness for spiders. I like the way they weave and how they homestead the sky. Tom likes their dietary savvy, which makes them important to his trade. Spiders are his taste-testers. He feeds them all sorts of bugs, and if they refuse to eat one, he asks himself why. This is "why" with a capital *W*, the sort of question whose answer will lead to other questions and other answers, and be useful in chemical prospecting. Tomorrow we plan to visit some of his royal taste-testers. So, bidding Tom good night, I return to the dormitory on the second floor of the main building and read a little before going to sleep. The book I've borrowed from a station intern is *Leave Me Never*, by Suzanne Carey, a steamy Silhouette Desire bodice ripper set at Archbold Station. Laughing at such sentences as "Before she could cry out or even speak, his other arm had come crushingly around her, pulling her up against the remembered male length of him," I finally fall asleep, thinking about the codes of courtship preferred by humans and fireflies.

After breakfast the next morning, Tom, Maria, Mark Deyrup (another entomologist), and I set out for Highland Hammock, an island of dense vegetation about an hour's drive north. Because Tom is intrigued by the orange-and-brown-spotted ornate moth, which may contain a drug useful to humans, we're going to do some experiments involving spiders. En route, we stop along the roadside and stroll in the brush, hoping to be lucky enough to find one of the endangered Tequesta scrub grasshoppers Mark is studying. This season he has already walked hundreds of miles along these highways and found precious few of them for study. A zebra swallowtail flutters across our path like a piece of newsprint, seemingly oblivious to the whoosh of traffic only a few yards away. The four-lane superhighway creates its own jet streams, transporting careless insects to who knows where.

"I think I see one," Maria calls. We hurry toward her with careful steps. Her keen eyes have zeroed in on a tiny twitch of black and white spots under a thatch of grass. The insect we're searching for is wingless, but it can hop quite a distance, thanks to powerful leg muscles. Maria glues her gaze to the bouncing grasshopper, pointing at it, hop by hop, until Mark catches it in his hands.

"Pretty big fellow," he says, turning it over. "Actually it's a female."

We huddle round him to have a closer look at the tiny black-and-white creature, which is both striped and spotted. In profile, it looks like a graph.

"The female is larger than the male," Mark explains, "and she tapers at one end. She lays her eggs underground, so she has these complicated little trowels at the rear end."

Bending down for a closer look, I follow her golden belly to a tiny pair of diggers. Then I look at the two compound eyes, surprised to discover black and white spots running right through them, too. Each domed eye is composed of hundreds of clear facets, in which the polka dots seem suspended.

"One of the peculiar things about scrub grasshoppers," Mark says, "is that they stay in coitus for many hours. You'll see them hopping around together, attached."

"Ultimate togetherness," Tom says. "They're *an item*." Maria laughs; it was only yesterday that Tom and Maria first heard that expression about a twosome and they like the late-breaking-news sound of it.

"How long do they live?" I ask.

"Almost a year," Mark says as we climb into the car, put the grasshopper safely away, and continue our drive. "But it's hard to study their relationships because ridges of scrub are sometimes isolated from each other by highways, housing tracts, orange groves. But grasshoppers seem to change genital shape very readily, and we can use that to identify which ones have been living close together and which ones have traveled. See, with insects, there's something called runaway evolution. Genitals change very fast within a group. It's apparently based on female preference. One group will develop a few little extra prongs on the male genitalia, although there's nothing particularly adaptive about them."

"If they don't help the animal adapt to its environment, why do they develop?"

"Just because the females like them. A little prong starts for some reason; the females prefer the prongs and mate with those males; and the offspring carry genes for prongs. You know, it may not be too different from the way the Irish elk became extinct— because the females kept saying, 'I don't want you until you get even bigger antlers.' Ultimately, the antlers got too big to carry."

One might wonder why female grasshoppers prefer the prongs in the first place. But nobody really knows. One theory is that it's very important for females to know that they actually have mated. The males have to transmit clearly the message that copulation has taken place. Among insects, copulation often gets interrupted by predators, weather, and so on. So it's important that both partners realize sperm has been transferred. If a male stimulates a female using a lot of ballyhoo or a novel design, he'll succeed in procreating, because the female will be absolutely sure copulation took place and will therefore reject other males. There's no point in her spending a lot of time mating if it's not necessary. These genital changes become extraordinarily elaborate and can involve bundles of hair, little growths of hooks, peculiar reversible sacs with hairs on the end, and unusual knobs that point in opposite directions. They're adaptive only in the sense that they assure the female that she's mating with a male of the right species, but they have no external use at all. They're just decorative. So, it's highly unlikely that different species would develop exactly the same genitals. This fact alone allows scientists to trace the relatedness of organisms and their habitats.

"Tom and I are very different entomologists," Mark continues. "A lot of his work has an old-fashioned natural-history base, but he's in the vanguard of what's being discovered now. Almost nothing that I do couldn't have been done a hundred years ago."

"Both of us have been dragged kicking and screaming into the nineteenth century," Tom corrects him.

"No, my kind of work is catching-up work. A lot of the natural-history and survey studies that took place in Europe in the eighteen-hundreds were never done in Florida. People were busy doing other things. So I spend a lot of time just listing insects, finding out where they live, how they live. It's not something that you can be paid to do."

When we think of science, we often picture arcane quests after minutiae, or efforts to explain underlying principles. But it's amazing that in a civilization as complex as ours, we are still engaged in Adam's task, the naming of the animals.

"There are very few places where you can actually look at a whole ecosystem and say how many of something live there," Mark says. "At the station, we're beginning to be able to do that. We've just put together a new moth-and-butterfly list, for instance, with more than eleven hundred species on it. And there's another five hundred or so species to be identified—that's just moths and butterflies! We have roughly nine hundred species of beetles listed, but we assume there are about two thousand. And the ants, bees, and wasps probably make up an even larger group. We've listed about one thousand flies. So the total number of different kinds of insects in Archbold's small habitat is about ten thousand. And that's nothing compared with what you'd find in a deciduous forest. The Endangered Species List is barely a start. Most insects aren't even known. So how can we tell which ones are endangered?"

Soon we arrive at Highland Hammock, a state park. As we walk along carefully laid-out pathways, we enjoy the primal feel of the dense forest, which contains a mix of northern and southern trees: vast woods of sweet gums and hackberries, red maples, hickories, and live oaks and pines. Flowering poison ivy vines twenty feet long hang from branches, with Spanish moss, epiphytes, and orchids. Flexing open a broad palmetto leaf, I see four species of moths, whose caterpillars are feeding on the leaves; wasp and fly parasites that attack the caterpillars; miscellaneous spiders, which coexist perfectly well with the moth caterpillars; parasites that attack the spiders; small millipedes; yellow ants; and fly maggots. On this one leaf, three feet above the ground, a complex ecosystem thrives. These are not creatures that one would find in the normal leaf litter on the forest floor, which is filled with other spiders, ants, and centipedes and is a dangerous place to live. Instead, these insects raise their generations on a sort of penthouse forest floor. It's odd to think of there being a specialized habitat no larger than a palmetto leaf.

"Aha!" Tom calls gleefully.

We find him up the road a few yards, happily inspecting a huge spiderweb, billowing at eye level between two trees. A big furry spider with a crazy-eight-shaped body and eight many-knuckled legs sits in the upper-right-hand corner of the web. Tom takes a vial out of his pocket, pulls an ornate moth from it, and tosses the moth onto the web. In a flash, the spider rappels down the silk and cages the moth in its legs.

"So much for the moth," I sigh.

"Wait." Tom raises a cautionary finger, as the spider begins cutting the moth loose from the web, using sharp fangs at either side of her mouth. "See, she's decided she doesn't want it. See how she backed away? Now the question is how she will treat it. She's cutting—see the cutting? There are two palps, which are like two short hands around the mouth—if we had palps, we could eat and play music at the same time!—and she's taking the thread with those two palps and putting it in her mouth. It's going to be cut loose in a second. Now she's starting to pull back so the moth doesn't damage more of the web."

The spider cuts a perfect window in the web with her sharp fangs. Playing doggo, the moth finally falls free and takes flight. Then the spider returns to her watch at the top of the web.

"Good heavens. Why did she do that? I thought spiders liked moths."

"Only edible ones," Tom says.

"Even so, why clip it from the web?"

"Because the spider can't see everywhere at once on a big web. So she takes the high ground and waits. When something vibrates the web, she can read the vibrations to tell exactly where it is. But if her web is cluttered with debris, she'll get a faulty signal."

I picture pilots jamming radar by dropping tinfoil in World War II. "How come the moth didn't try to escape?"

"Because it didn't have a damn thing to worry about. Instead of fluttering in the web, it lets the spider do the work."

In the sunlight, this golden-web spider's shimmery silk stands out brightly. Touching one thread with his fingertip, Tom pulls it farther and farther to show how it can stretch. A spider spins different kinds of silk for different parts of a web; stretchy threads have more water in them. The silk at the center of the web is so elastic that, when an insect falls in and flails, it's essentially kicking against rubber bands. A struggling insect never really puts tension on the web; it just wraps itself up tighter.

"The elasticity of these threads is unbelievably mysterious," Tom says admiringly. "There isn't a single human synthetic material that has that kind of elasticity. It's better than rubber, and the toughness is out-of-sight." He plucks at the silk.

"Why isn't the spider running down to your forceps?"

"A big movement like that? She knows exactly what fight to pick. And she has all sorts of strategies. If I touch the web too hard, she has lots of escape routes and will know just where to go. But I don't want to freak her out. She's a nice little gal."

Nearby, a small white orchid hangs from a branch. Everywhere one turns are curiosities involving insects. Many species of orchid almost never produce seeds and even act as if they don't want to be fertilized; they don't produce any nectar to seduce an insect. On rare occasions, though, an inexperienced insect may stumble into one by mistake and smear pollen around. Then the orchid produces thousands of seeds, and in that hit-or-miss way it survives. Nectar is cheap for a flower to make, and yet hundreds of species of orchids are unappetizingly dry. It's a mystery how they survive in a relationship that relies so much on accident. But somehow they manage, thanks to the bumbling of insects.

Experiments must be repeatable and include a control group, so Tom has brought two flavors of ornate moth—a naturally poisonous one (it gets that way because its caterpillars feed on a deadly variety of pea plant) and a harmless one raised on poison-free food. Time after time, the spiders devour the safe moths and release the toxic ones. When we're content with the evidence, we head back to the station to get a second opinion from equally picky eaters—the endangered Florida scrub jays.

Back at camp, Tom adjusts the focus on a large gray Wild microscope set up in the laboratory room of his cottage. "Romance," he says. Although there was no spoken beginning to the sentence, he concludes the one unfolding in his mind: ". . . and deceit."

The insect world is storied with seduction, deception, and death. When he passes a moth to me, I hold it under the microscope and peer at its beautiful pattern. Suddenly two pinkish-yellow feather dusters unfurl from its rear end.

"Amazing! What are *they*?"

Tom takes a look. "Scent brushes," he says. "Males use them in courtship. They're actually modified scales, and each one is hollow and perforated."

"Like a straw?"

"Very much. Vapor rises up each of the hairs on the brush. One day I saw one of these guys fly into a spiderweb. I knew that moths usually flutter themselves loose, leaving some of their scales behind, but this moth simply folded its wings and played dead. The spider came up, touched it, cut it free, and it fell to the ground. I didn't think much about it. Then a year later I saw exactly the same phenomenon, and I decided I'd better take a look at the moth. I found out that as a caterpillar, the moth feeds on a poisonous pea plant. So I tried to see if I could raise the caterpillar on a synthetic, poison-free diet, and it worked. We knew that the pea plant had a certain type of alkaloid that is very toxic to humans. Every once in a while cows browse on these plants and die. It's a liver poison, really bad stuff. Comfrey tea, which I don't think is used anymore, had the same poison in it. But this alkaloid turns out to be distasteful to spiders. Any animal that can feed on these plants with impunity has got it made, because it can build up a storehouse of poison in its own body and use it for defense. And that's the strategy of these moths."

"So they consume it, and it saturates their body. Why don't they die from it?"

"Great question," he says excitedly, his voice making it clear that in his private vocabulary, "question" means the same as "puzzle." "It turns out that when you eat these chemicals, you don't actually eat them as poison—you eat a chemical your liver converts into a poison. And that needs certain enzymes. I think what the moth has done is shut off that kind of enzymatic system so it can take these chemicals in and not convert them, and thus use them the same way the plant does. That's really very clever.

"So out we came with moths raised on a poison-free diet. We spent the whole damn winter raising these moths. We wanted to see whether they would be palatable to spiders. We threw them in spiderwebs, and one after another they got eaten by the spiders. I felt as if I was seventeen, on my first date, and had just got my first kiss. It was mind-boggling.

"Then I decided to look into the courtship of the moths. We knew that the males have these nifty scent brushes that they pull out for courtship. And we knew that the females attract the males. The female sits on the plant, and the males hover and fly very slowly in one direction. If you follow their line of flight, you can find the female moth that does the calling."

"How does this siren moth call? With scent?"

"She makes an aphrodisiac in a special gland in her abdomen. I gave extracts from those glands to Jerry Meinwald, and in due course Jerry and his people came up with a formula. Actually, there are three compounds in there, all simple hydrocarbon

straight-chain molecules with little bonds in them, all sex attrac-
tants. We sometimes take that chemical and put it out in traps to
bring in males. This is not a long-distance attractant, but it doesn't
need to be. A few yards is all that's needed, since a moth may
spend its entire life in or near one plant.

"When the male is in range of the female, fluttering around her,
those brushes come out in a fraction of a second—once, twice,
three, four times as he flies around her," Tom says, making a slow
circle with one closed hand, which he opens slowly to mimic the
unfolding brushes. "But there was one question that bothered me
in particular. I wanted to know who was in control of this
courtship. Was it the male? If so, then it was a case of metabolic
expedience. The male has a useful chemical, some of which he uses
for defense; the rest he converts into a chemical that works to
seduce the female. Sounds good. But suppose instead this was
really a female choice."

"You mean he would advertise how much defensive chemical
he has?"

"That's exactly what ended up being the case. And I remember
the moment that occurred to me. I was feeding otters in California.
A question was bothering me: Was there some subtle thing that the
moth could accomplish by using a derivative of this alkaloid? And
the idea came to me that this wasn't a case of seducing the female
at all. It just looked like seduction. It was in fact that the male had
to prove his worth to the female in some way. It was the female
who was choosy."

"So she wants a warrior?"

"She wants to have some evidence that he's worth his salt, or
whatever the insect equivalent is."

"But he's proving he has enough defensive chemical to protect
him."

"That's what I thought at first, that the male was flexing his
muscles, saying, 'If you take me as your husband, your sons and
daughters are going to be good at getting a lot of alkaloid out of
the plant. The more they have of it, the better defended they'll be.
And this will make them better able to compete with other larvae
on the food plant for seeds. And wouldn't you like to have a suitor
who can prove to you that he is genetically fit?' Well, we published

that interpretation, and we were very proud of ourselves. But then the story got even better. We found that the egg of this animal also has alkaloid in it. So we assumed that the female actually laid eggs with alkaloid. But how does it get there? The male must transmit some of this stuff to the female with the sperm."

Male insects often ejaculate vitamin gifts into the female along with their sperm, to make sure the offspring will have nutrients on which to grow. I remember being able to feel those ball-bearing-like packages in the soft bellies of pregnant monarch butterflies when I was tagging them in California. Insects produce some of the largest sperm packages in the world relative to their body mass. There are male beetles that donate as much as 10 percent of their body weight.

Turning away from the microscope, Tom warms to the telling of his Kiplingesque story. "Well, it turns out that the females say, 'Look, I'm putting all the yolk into these eggs. What are you going to do for your offspring?' So we thought maybe the male was in effect saying to the female, 'Not only do I come from a lineage that's good in competing for the seeds from the food plant, but I'm also willing to give you direct payment in the form of a gift with which you can enrich your own defenses, or you can put some of it in your eggs to protect them, or both.' And that turned out to be the case. The amount of alkaloid transferred by the male to the female is proportional to the amount of alkaloid that the male has, which is in turn proportional to the amount of scent that he produces on his scent brushes. In other words, he really is telling the female exactly how much he's got in his bank account."

"Call me a cynic, but why wouldn't it be in his best interest to lie?"

"You tell me. Of course, we can't say categorically that some don't lie. For example, if a male has very little alkaloid, could he convert it all to the scent message on the brushes and dupe the female into thinking that he has a big bank account? In theory, I suppose. But they really don't appear to be lying. And if they don't appear to lie, it can only be because it doesn't pay off. They must get found out in some way. The next question in this courtship drama is how they get found out. Is it possible that the female might be able to check after mating if he was a liar, and discriminate against the sperm? We don't know."

"It sounds as if only the muscle men win in this scenario."

"Not always. At one point, we released males into the field (just like the ones you saw with the spider today). Some had alkaloid, some didn't—in other words, some with scent on their brushes and some without. We wing-notched them all so we'd recognize them; baited them with sexy females we knew would start broadcasting at a certain time of the night; convinced the females to sit on a little wire perch, which we treated chemically with an extract of the pea plant to make it more attractive for them to sit on; and then waited. A male would come in and court. We recognized the male by the wing-notching, so we knew whether he had alkaloid or not. Males with the alkaloid had about a thirty-percent higher chance of being accepted. That's a major edge. If you have a thirty-percent higher chance of fathering offspring, that's quite an advantage. But it's not that the ones without alkaloid got turned away. The female can get sperm from the male, but she also has to take a big gamble and ask herself, 'Is this the last male I'm likely to attract in the next five days? What do I do?' At the very least, she can get nutrients from a sperm package. So she mates with up to thirteen different males, gets nutrients from all of them, and also tries to mate with as many of the ones who'll give her the alkaloid defense as possible."

How does she carry around all that booty, I wonder. "Doesn't she get awfully heavy?"

"Yes. But she's also laying eggs."

"So she'll be inseminated, lay eggs, be inseminated, lay eggs?"

"Lay *some* eggs. In fact, we know that if she gets inseminated by two males, she doesn't lay half the eggs from the first male, half from the second. No, she will lay eggs from one male only. After mating she's still putting the male to the test in other ways. The eggs will be sired by the largest stud. How does she tell the largest stud? Probably from the size of the sperm package. It's mind-boggling. And the interesting thing is that the size of the male is proportional to the amount of the alkaloid he carries. It's truth in advertising. So before mating she's asking him, 'Hey, how much alkaloid do you have?' And after mating she's double-checking him on the size of the sperm package."

"Just leafing through the bills, to make sure all the fives and tens are there?"

"Exactly."

Over a hundred years ago, Darwin was speculating about intrigues like this one, which involve female choice and sexual selection. He wondered if, since the female really puts so much investment into the offspring, she might not be the choosy one.

"The male strategy, almost always, is to inseminate as many females as possible, without paying much attention to them. But there are some exceptions. For example, I once worked on a beetle that ejects the equivalent of half the weight of the eggs that the female will produce. So it's really a major contribution. And sure enough, the female has a way of conning something from the male—a gift—and then not letting him inseminate her. This female can't mate more than once every so many days, but she tries to get gifts from males anyway. A male doesn't want to give her gifts if she's carrying another male's offspring. So he goes around to the rear end of the female, which she tries to prevent, and smells her to see if she's a virgin, something he prizes very highly."

"What a complex courtship."

"People have this idea that human predicaments are too complicated for an insect. Nonsense! There's an enormous amount of biology you can pack into something the size of an insect. The only reason we know so little about them is that they're so small."

"I wonder how people would respond to insects if insects were larger—say, the size of dogs and cats."

"It all depends on whether people grew up with negative ideas about insects. If the world was full of huge grasshoppers, leaping around at the speed they actually do, carrying the momentum that they do, they'd be bloody hazardous. I tell you, suits of armor would still be very fashionable. Moms would say, 'Don't forget your suit of armor, dear—the grasshoppers are out!' "

The ornate moth saga is one of Tom's favorites. He's been studying its habits for twenty years and always discovering something new. Although he's usually working on a number of insect stories—sometimes just by being alert to them—one theme running through them is female choice.

"Is it possible to study insect societies and not extrapolate to humans?" I ask.

"I'm a dyed-in-the-wool sociobiologist," he says, laughing. "It's not surprising to me that much of what the human animal does can be described in animal terms."

"Like giving big engagement rings?"

"Sure. Our whole courtship story can be told romantically, of course—clothing it in cultural traditions, if you wish—but the fundamental biology is that individuals are trying to perpetuate their genes in the next generation. The female is fundamentally choosy, which makes darn good sense if you're going to sit on an egg for nine months. The male doesn't want to waste his seed, as they say in the Bible."

"So she tests him in various ways."

"Absolutely. And that gets built into the culture—the whole idea of the athlete, the winner, the contests, the warrior. I can't explain it all, but I have absolute faith that biological thinking is at the root of everything we do as humans."

"Sometimes people think of insects as cold-blooded automatons. Comparing any of our actions with theirs then becomes doubly frightening."

"The concept of free will is so fundamental. Do we have free will or don't we? I don't worry much about that, because I'm so absolutely fascinated by entering the world of another species and trying to figure out what they do. As someone who is not religious, who doesn't believe in free will in the traditional way, who believes in evolution, and that we're part of the evolutionary process, I still consider us to be unique in the sense that we can sit here and talk about it and understand it. But we're clearly not unique in terms of what we do with our muscles; we're not unique in what we do with our gametes when we're mating; we're not unique when we're part of a courtship strategy that involves female choosiness. In those ways, we're just animals of a different sort, ones with four fewer legs than insects."

A knock at the door summons us, and we see a tall, chestnut-haired woman in a sweater and pants standing next to a man of about the same height, whose hair is tied back in a ponytail. Tom introduces us, and I'm delighted to discover they're the nature photographers Susan Middleton and David Liittschwager, who are busy locating and photographing a host of endangered animals and plants. On a three-year journey around the United States, they are visually cataloguing our vanishing life-forms. Tom is looking forward to studying the grasshopper we found this morning, but he's also excited that Susan and David will record it for posterity.

"We're on our way to shoot some jays," Susan explains. "We found a great spot yesterday. Want to drive out with us?"

"Absolutely!" Tom says. "Let me grab some moths. Oh, by the way," he adds excitedly, "we've got the grasshopper for you."

Susan and David cheer, and start planning their evening's work as I help Tom pluck live ornate moths from a cage and tuck them, all silk and flutter, into separate vials. Then we climb into the Land Rover and head for the end of the station. David drives with a slightly maniacal grin; when the road becomes a river of deep, wallowy sand, the four-wheel drive is all slither and swerve for fifteen minutes.

At last we park in a maze of dwarf oak trees and clean white sand. Because the trees are roughly at eye level, it is like wandering through a scene from Shakespeare—you hear voices but can't see the speakers, and they, in turn, don't know you're there. All around us, the Florida scrub is picture-perfect, even if its name suggests that it's useless, disposable land. The scrub is an area that has deep, sterile sand. Fire and soil forge an elemental relationship that has survived for ages. One of its attractions is that, in so simple a landscape, the concerns of organisms are easy to spot. Although sand is at its heart, it's like other simple habitats elsewhere. New York City, for example, has a lot of wild plants and insects caught between two millstones: the concrete and the unrelenting human activity. Those insects are interesting because they've coped with overwhelming environmental factors. Life in the scrub is similar, chastened by the tremendous sterility of the area, the lack of water in the winter, and the fires that sweep it over and over again, century after century. Many of the insect species came originally from savanna areas around the Gulf of Mexico at the end of the Pliocene, along with all sorts of antelopes, giant gophers, tortoises, and ground sloths. Many of these animals died out elsewhere, but on the scrub ridges, where the sand is deep and sterile and dries out fast, western creatures survived. So the scrub has become a home to organisms that are very old and strange. Now they remain only on the tops of a few ridges. The scrub itself is endangered. All we have left is the Atlantic coastal ridge, which is much younger than this inland ridge; Lake Wales ridge; Marian uplands; a very thin band of scrub in the Panhandle; and little knolls of scrub in small areas in western Florida. A tiny bit of Panhandle scrub works its way into Georgia and Alabama, but scrubland is almost totally Floridian. And there are many creatures unique to the Florida scrub.

One endangered resident is the scrub jay, which is in trouble because it requires large areas of land over which to roam—each jay family needs about twenty acres. They can't mate within the family (as insects can), so there must be many other families around. Even though they're long-lived birds, well adjusted to scrub, they have become a very small population. Thousands of other species ride in the media wake of the jays. Just as golden lion tamarins are the cute and cuddly poster animals of the Mata Atlantica rain forest in Brazil, the jays symbolize the plight of scrub habitat. People find them easier to identify with than insects, snakes, or trees. Northern crested blue jays are tough, hoodlum birds with bad tempers; they're street-corner bullies. But scrub jays are smaller, gentler, more like the bluebird of cartoon and song. The unstated agenda of any "Save the Jays" campaign is to save the habitat of the jays and all their less-photogenic neighbors.

A flock of blue wheels low over the maze of dwarf oaks in which we stand. They look like falling shards of sky. For many years, Archbold researchers have been banding and studying these jay families, so the birds aren't frightened of us. Dressed in Civil War colors, the scrub jay has a blue helmet and blue wing and tail feathers, but its chest, chin hairs, and eyebrows are gray. Acorns and insects are its favorite fare. Tom pulls a vial from one of his many pockets, removes a moth, and holds it in the air. A jay glides down and lands on his raised arm, hops to his wrist, tightens its grappling-hook feet, and turns an eye to the moth, perhaps smelling it. Then it flies away. We try the experiment again. Pulling a moth carefully from a vial, I hold it aloft. Three jays bicker as they approach. One lands at the base of my thumb, wrapping a claw tightly around it. When it leans over to inspect the moth, its soft belly brushes my skin. The feathers are so delicate they ignite nerve cells in only a tiny patch of skin, and yet my whole body responds to that rare touch. Its body does, too. The jay cocks its head sideways and stares at me, one eye like a rebus. Then it watches the moth as intently as I am watching the jay. Deciding that the moth is inedible, the jay flies off. Tom smiles. There is definitely a powerful drug in that moth. Spiders won't eat it and birds won't eat it. A bag of ornate moths will become part of the bio-treasure-chest he sends to Merck for analysis.

Soon the sun burns fiercely off the sand, so we head back to camp for shade and lunch. While the others go to their cottages, I climb the water tower's spiral staircase. The wind surf grows louder as I climb away from all the cozy details of the human world, up 146 silver-coated steps. At the top, I find a platform swaying gently, red plastic streamers fluttering from a turret, and a wasp whose fiefdom I've breached. Below stands the main building with its chamois-colored stucco, red slate roof, and six rooflets running south like cresting waves. The noon sun cuts triangular sails under the eaves, and the long building seems to float on the vast ocean of scrub.

Tom is most likely in his cottage, working on an upcoming lecture. In a few weeks, he will testify before the U.S. Senate, asking it to reauthorize the Endangered Species Act. He has spent his life probing barely visible worlds, but it's a far cry from explorer to counsel, from rapt devotee to public defender. He plans to recite a long list of medicines derived from plants and animals, and to point out that most species have never been investigated. Although our culture is embarrassed by goods that are "worn out," there is no such thing as chemical obsolescence. So he'll caution the senators that even if an insect has been carefully studied for chemical assets and has been found lacking, it shouldn't be dismissed as of no interest and allowed to become extinct, because it may contain a wealth of chemicals that can be discovered by future techniques. He'll stress that it's no use raising insects in captivity for this purpose, because they've evolved to produce chemicals in response to trials they encounter in the wild. Therefore an endangered habitat like the Florida scrub must be saved, if only for the sake of the unique insects it supports. He will tell his tales of fireflies, ornate moths, and bombardier beetles—favorite stories that involve familiar, nonthreatening bugs. Since chemical prospecting is so lucrative, the senators stand to profit mightily while looking virtuous. Some will vote green for altruistic reasons, some may have other motives, but all will *appear* altruistic, and that's fine with Tom. In politics, as in insect society, virtue is never its own reward.

Two humans stroll languidly toward the dining hall. I think they are male and female, but I can't see their faces well enough to know if they're clean-shaven or wearing makeup, how they style their hair, what they carry in their pockets. Astronauts returning from orbit have marveled at how little of human life can be seen from space—not the wars or political boundaries, not the cities or farms, not the subtleties of custom, adolescence, or love. Strolling farther away, the couple seem to shrink as they cross the veranda together. Suddenly, the male raises his chin and grins; his teeth flash in the sunlight. The female crosses her hands high on her chest, stoops briefly from the waist, and twists her face; her teeth flash, too. Then the male bows at an angle, swings his head up, and opens his mouth. I assume that he said something funny, to which she replied with something funny, and that led to this suite of laughing bows. Are they *an item*? Are they colleagues? Have they spent the morning working or making love? From this height, I can't begin to understand their complex relationship, any more than humans peering down at insects can know how complicated *their* lives are. So much slips through the seams of our senses. Involved in a conversation older than words, the two humans enter the building to dine, out of hunger, like any lark or beetle.

Lake Placid lies in the distance, a puddle of mercury. The scrub looks stark, exhausted, and uninhabited: the environmental equivalent of an empty lot. And yet I know that millions of animals are going about their daily chores down there, caught up in acts of murder, marriage, feast, birth. Countless life-and-death dramas are playing themselves out. But much is lost to the naked eye. There are marauding bands of hunters; sculptors of leaf and bark; some of the first papermakers on earth; rustlers and ranchers with their own stockyards; gatherers of fruit and petal; architects working in clay; nurseries for the young; catacombs, lean-tos, and towers; weavers of silk and cotton; builders of cities; practitioners of order; many different tribes and societies. All these can tumble in the throes of a storm, or when giants walk among them. What a shame we seldom behold their wondrous cities. Looking out over the scrub, silently praising their hidden world, I remember with what conviction Walt Whitman once wrote, "The bright suns I see and the dark suns I cannot see are in their place."

INDEX

Poet, essayist, and naturalist, DIANE ACKERMAN was born in Waukegan, Illinois. She received M.A., M.F.A., and Ph.D. degrees from Cornell University. Her poetry has been published in leading literary journals and in her books *The Planets: A Cosmic Pastoral, Wife of Light, Lady Faustus, Reverse Thunder: A Dramatic Poem,* and *Jaguar of Sweet Laughter: New and Selected Poems.*

Her works of nonfiction include, most recently, *A Natural History of Love*; the critically acclaimed *The Moon by Whale Light, and Other Adventures Among Bats, Crocodilians, Penguins, and Whales*; *On Extended Wings,* her memoir of flying; *Monk Seal Hideaway,* her first children's book; and the best-selling *A Natural History of the Senses.*

Ms. Ackerman has received many prizes and awards. In 1994 she was honored as a Literary Lion by the New York Public Library. She has taught at a variety of universities, including Columbia and Cornell. Her essays about nature and human nature have appeared in *National Geographic, The New Yorker, The New York Times, Parade,* and other journals. A five-hour PBS television series inspired by *A Natural History of the Senses* aired in 1995, with Ms. Ackerman as host.

This book was set in Sabon, a typeface designed by the well-known German typographer Jan Tschichold (1902–74). Sabon's design is based upon the original letter forms of Claude Garamond and was created specifically to be used for three sources: foundry type for hand composition, Linotype, and Monotype. Tschichold named his typeface for the famous Frankfurt typefounder Jacques Sabon, who died in 1580.